Principled Persuasion in Employee Communication

I've consulted with many large household name enterprises over the years and seen both highly effective and ineffective styles of internal communication. This deep and erudite book sets out to persuade you to rethink the old approaches and communicate creatively with employees, so they can better contribute to common goals. I strongly recommend all senior executives to read this book!

Graham Tomkinson, CEO Performance Brunel; formerly COO of IBM's European Management Consulting Division

Wonderfully disturbing and inspiringly constructive, Principled Persuasion in Employee Communication is both a critique of current practice in organisational communications and a vision of its possibilities. Informed by history, philosophy, psychology, ethics, science and technology, Mike Churchman offers a provocative and compelling argument for why the price of engineered, top-down communication is no longer worth paying and needs to give way to more dynamic, progressive and collaborative patterns. Principled Persuasion in Employee Communication is a manifesto for the long-awaited revolution which could see organisations finally combine both productivity and humanity.

Alan Robertson, Director, Business Cognition Ltd

This is an interesting analysis of developments in the way that organisations are managed and the impact on internal communication. It presents a well-argued case, steeped in references to psychology, for a new open, truthful and ethical approach to internal communication and a good life at work. An excellent guide to help internal communication practitioners and operational managers make organisations a more meaningful place for people to work.

Kevin Ruck, Co-founder, The PR Academy

Principled Persuasion in Employee Communication

MIKE CHURCHMAN

GOWER

Published by
Gower Publishing Limited
Wey Court East
Union Road
Farnham
Surrey, GU9 7PT
England

Gower Publishing Company
110 Cherry Street
Suite 3-1
Burlington
VT 05401-3818
USA

www.gowerpublishing.com

Mike Churchman has asserted his right under the Copyright, Designs and Patents Act, 1988, to be identified as the author of this work.

British Library Cataloguing in Publication Data
A catalogue record for this book is available from the British Library.

ISBN: 9781472475060 (pbk)
ISBN: 9781472475077 (ebk – PDF)
ISBN: 9781472475084 (ebk ePUB)

Library of Congress Cataloging-in-Publication Data
Churchman, Mike.
  Principled persuasion in employee communication / by Mike Churchman.
    pages cm
  Includes bibliographical references and index.
  ISBN 978-1-4724-7506-0 (pbk) -- ISBN 978-1-4724-7507-7 (ebook) --
  ISBN 978-1-4724-7508-4 (epub) 1. Leadership. 2. Interpersonal
  communication. 3. Persuasion (Psychology) I. Title.
  HM1261.C48 2016
  303.3'4--dc23

                                                    2015020654

Printed in the United Kingdom by Henry Ling Limited, at the Dorset Press, Dorchester, DT1 1HD

Contents

PART IV   NEXT STEPS

Introduction

The young discipline of employee communication has reached a turning point. Should it continue to operate as an arm of command and control? Or should it transform itself into a positive force for good, freeing up employees to flourish as individuals? When you look at what's going to happen in the world of work in the next few decades, it becomes clear there are two possible pathways.

One leads to an ENGINEERED ORGANISATION where command and control will be powerfully enhanced by technologies that monitor and record every action carried out by employees. This type of organisation will continue to use Motivational Communication to exert control over employees from within their own minds, using language designed to inculcate prescribed values.

The other leads to a PROGRESSIVE ORGANISATION where high levels of free and open communication will stimulate innovation and make work more pleasurable. In this type of organisation, employee communication will take the form of Principled Persuasion, the aim of which is to create happier, less harmful and more ethical working environments, using language that's clear, meaningful, rhetorically powerful and truthful.

In ENGINEERED ORGANISATIONS employees will continue to be part of a machine, valued only for their output, though this fact will be disguised by propaganda. In PROGRESSIVE ORGANISATIONS all employees will be valued for what they are, resourceful, creative, unique human beings capable of making a serious contribution to the organisation's strategy.

In making the turn from Motivational Communication to Principled Persuasion, the young discipline of employee communication will begin to grow up and mature. Principled Persuaders, not accountants, are likely to be the CEOs of the future as persuasive communication takes centre stage as the driving force behind organisational success.

Make no mistake, most organisations have totally underrated the strategic importance of employee communication. Despite some advances, few have encouraged the spread of communication skills throughout the workforce. Principled Persuaders understand that the key to dealing with the unpredictable events about to unfold in the twenty-first century will be a new way of communicating with the workforce. The flexibility, adaptability and innovation that will be needed to survive and prosper in coming decades can only be achieved by liberating employees, not imprisoning them further in established systems and processes.

So that's what this book is all about. How and why employee communication needs to change from Motivational Communication into Principled Persuasion in order to create PROGRESSIVE ORGANISATIONS.

You will see:

- How employee communication has evolved during the nineteenth and twentieth centuries and why it needs to move on from where it is now.
- How five converging forces will pose immense ethical and logistical challenges for organisations and why this will present leaders with a choice of two pathways to the future.
- How people's minds are fixed within their own views of the world and why open discussion is the best route to culture change.
- How there are six main sources of happiness at work and why employee happiness is a central aim of Principled Persuasion.
- How harmful acts and bad people get in the way of employee happiness and why Principled Persuasion needs to be used to minimise harms in the organisation.
- How it's possible to extract twelve lessons and four main principles from the story of Western ethics and why ethics should become a continual focus of discussion for all employees.
- How a better use of English can open up minds, introduce new ideas and stimulate conversations in the workplace and why it's critical that organisational language should become more meaningful and clear.
- How rhetoric can be reinstated as a force for good in organisations and why rhetorical communication is essential for nourishing the right culture.
- How the cancer of propaganda has eaten into employee communication and why it's so important for Principled Persuaders to tell the truth.
- How Principled Persuaders can begin taking practical steps towards creating progressive organisations and why this is the right way forward for the discipline of employee communication in the twenty-first century.

PART I
A CONTINUING JOURNEY

CHAPTER 1

Pathways from the Past: The Evolution of Employee Communication

History does not repeat itself, but it rhymes.[1]

What follows is a familiar story, but looked at from a different angle. It's a story of two mighty forces struggling with each other. It's a drama that continues to the present day. On one side are employers, intent on controlling their workers. On the other side are individual employees with a strong desire for more rewarding, happier lives at work. This tension between 'power from above' and 'power from below' will need to be resolved in the twenty-first century.

As you'll see, internal communication from management down to employees has evolved as an arm of command and control. Feeding off emerging theories about how people think, in the late twentieth century the art of persuasion in organisations took the form of Motivational Communication. In this chapter, I'm going to show you how this happened by looking at the evolution of employee communication in the nineteenth and twentieth centuries.

Let's start by taking an overview. On the next page you will find a summary of the evolution of employee communication. You can see the 'milestones', the big step-changes that have taken place over the years, the effect they had on employee communication, and a broad timeline.[2] We'll use these milestones as a structure for this chapter.

---

1   Attributed to Mark Twain.
2   To my knowledge, no full history has been written on the subject of employee communications. This would be a fascinating subject for a PhD, especially if it took international differences of approach into account.

The Evolution of Employee Communication

Milestone	Impact on employee communication	Timeline
Arrival of large-scale production and standardisation	Instruction on how to make products and supervision	Late eighteenth century
Standard products made by machines	Inculcation of the Christian work ethic	Early nineteenth century onwards
Very large organisations begin to form	Paternalistic – company newspapers – works councils	Mid nineteenth century onwards
Scientific management is introduced	Instruction on how to carry out specific actions and supervision	Early twentieth century
The rise of industrial psychology	Understanding dawns that workers have minds of their own	1920s/1930s
Theories of how to motivate workers begin to emerge	Attention paid to 'management styles'	1940s–1960s
The post-war golden age of full employment and the rise of planning	Communication dominated by unions, the collective voice, 'us' and 'them'	1950s–1970s
Managements begin to use communication to motivate employees and improve performance	Shift from internal PR to internal marketing – missions, visions and the language of empowerment	1980s–1990s
New communication channels expand rapidly	Employee communication becomes strategic – the language of engagement	2000–2020

Command and Control

Before the nineteenth century, the lives of most working people were spent in the fields or the household. Craftsmen and 'journeymen', the core labourers, were relatively independent. They were multi-taskers, able to design, make and set tools, and complete the whole job. For most workers, the relationship with the master, whether good or bad, would have been a close one. Communication between them was personal.

All this began to change by the middle of the eighteenth century. Large factories sprang up. In England by 1759, John Taylor's toy factory employed 600 people and, by 1770, Matthew Boulton's steam engine works had around 1,000 employees. The world's first mass consumer markets were beginning to appear and manufacturers were quick to spot the opportunities.

Take Josiah Wedgwood, for example. One of the pioneers of consumerism, he realised customers wanted crockery that exactly matched the products advertised in his catalogue. But maintaining consistency in pottery manufacture was seriously difficult. The workmanship of the individual potters varied considerably. Specialisation[3] had already taken hold in the potteries. One craftsman no longer had responsibility for all stages of manufacture; jobs were split into specific tasks. Yet the workers still had some control over the final appearance of the product.

Wedgwood took this control away by splitting the work into even more separate tasks. The craftsman's freedom to influence the final form of the pottery was completely eliminated. Designers determined style, colour and ornamentation. Men had to work to exact sets of instructions, carefully watched by supervisors. So by the late eighteenth century, a basic template of employee communication had been established. 'This is what you should do, this is how you should do it, and I'll be keeping an eye on you'. This is pure command and control – a simple formula that still applies in millions of workplaces across the world today.

Indoctrination

The next big step in the quick march of industrialisation was the manufacture of standard products by machine. The first products to be manufactured by machine in their entirety were ships' pulleys, in 1801.[4] The arrival of machines intensified the working day. Human beings became extensions of the machine. Masses of men, women and children were used up like raw material. In the nineteenth century, many employers had a total disregard for the biological limits of their workers.

---

3   Increasing specialisation has been one of the main driving forces behind economic growth. Adam Smith was quick to spot this. In his seminal book *The Wealth of Nations* he famously describes the principle of the division of labour in a pin-making factory: 'One man draws out the wire, another straights it, a third cuts it, a fourth points it, a fifth grinds it at the top for receiving the head … making a pin is, in this manner, divided into about eighteen distinct operations'. (Adam Smith, *The Wealth of Nations* (Penguin, 1999 [1776]), Book 1, Chapter 1, 110).

4   At the turn of the nineteenth century warships were dependent on sails whose proper functioning could involve up to a thousand pulleys on a single ship. For centuries, pulley blocks had been made, shaped and fitted entirely by hand. In 1801 the Royal Navy set up a manufacturing workshop with machines designed by Marc Isambard Brunel that turned out a range of consistent, 'standard' pulleys.

Employers, though, were assisted by a form of employee communication that took place well away from the factory floor, in church. Preachers taught that poorly paid and exhausted workers could expect their reward in heaven. Working people were instructed to be obedient to authority for the good of their souls. In the middle of the nineteenth century, a passer-by on a Sunday morning could hear the congregation singing 'All Things Bright and Beautiful', including the words:

> *The rich man in his castle,*
> *The poor man at his gate,*
> *God made them high and lowly,*
> *And ordered their estate.*

Even if they could afford to go to the music hall to relax, they had to listen to some cheery chappy singing:

> *So work boys work and be contented*
> *As long as you've enough to buy a meal*
> *The man you may rely, will be wealthy by and by*
> *If he'll only put his shoulder to the wheel.*[5]

The ethos of the time was 'stay in your place and do what your betters tell you to do'. Max Weber's identification and analysis of what came to be called the 'Protestant Work Ethic'[6] has been criticised for over-stating its effect. But it's impossible to understand why there was so little active resistance to terrible working conditions without taking into account that the workforce was being indoctrinated with Christian precepts. This ethic was based on the belief that hard work equated with piety, and material success in life could be seen as a sign of God's favour. By contrast, an unwillingness to work hard, and being in poverty, were seen as signs of a lack of inner grace. Slacking and idleness were deadly sins.

This belief system worked well for employers, who, after all, lived in a completely different world from their employees. Novelist and politician Benjamin Disraeli described the facts of social life. The nation, said one of his characters, is divided into rich and poor:

---

5   Words by Harry Clifton.
6   It wasn't just a Protestant work ethic. In the United States, the railway magnate, James J. Hill, built a Roman Catholic seminary to train priests who would preach virtues of diligence and respect for authority to his Irish immigrant labourers.

*between whom there is no intercourse and no sympathy; who are as
ignorant of each other's habits, thoughts and feelings as if they were
dwellers in different zones, or inhabitants of different planets; who
are formed by different breeding, are fed by different food, and are not
governed by the same laws.*[7]

Employee communication needs to be seen in its broader social context.
During the nineteenth century there's no doubt that religious indoctrination
helped to keep workers docile and compliant. Hard-pressed workers would
effectively 'police' themselves. And before you think this is all ancient history,
it's worth reflecting on the fact that employees are still surrounded by the quasi-
religious language of 'missions' and 'visions'. After all, today's Motivational
Communication sets out to 'align' employees and inculcate values that will
encourage them to be more committed and productive.

Paternalism

As the Industrial Revolution gathered speed and intensity, some employers saw
it as their duty to be kinder towards their workers. Prominent amongst this
type of employer were non-conformists such as Quakers, Congregationalists
and Unitarians. They felt a sense of Christian mission towards their employees,
which took the shape of a commitment to their social welfare. But there was a
sharper edge to their benevolence. They realised it made good business sense.
Looking after employees built loyalty to the company and its owners, as well as
reducing absenteeism and staff turnover. What's more, it fitted naturally into
the prevailing class system of deferential workers and superior bosses.

Many employers, large and small, encouraged their workers to feel part
of a 'family'. At Cadbury in England, for example, personal interactions
between bosses and workers, gifts and other signs of kindness helped to
create an environment in which employees could idealise 'Mr George'
and 'Mr Richard' as generous benefactors, even father figures. Paternalist
employers sought to promote good morals and habits of behaviour amongst
their workers, seeing them rather like children that needed to be brought
up properly.

In 1905, chocolate magnate, B. Seebohm Rowntree, expressed the view
that:

---

7   From Benjamin Disraeli's *Sybil* (1845), Book 2, Chapter 5.

> *Probably much more beneficial influence upon the character of the working classes may be exercised through the medium of their places of employment than is at present exercised by the churches.*[8]

There were significant and real benefits for workers in these more benevolent organisations. They introduced profit sharing, sickness and accident insurance and help with savings accounts. As organisations grew larger, the list of benefits expanded to encompass housing,[9] pensions, paid holidays, savings accounts, maternity homes, ophthalmic and dental clinics, sports clubs, recreation grounds, works dances, science classes and other educational programmes.

In these large organisations it became impossible for the employers to know their employees by name. Gone were the days when they could stroll about the factory floor to show the personal touch. By the late nineteenth century, 'house newspapers' appeared on the scene.[10] They were seen as a way of plugging the gap that had opened up between employers and their employees. They were filled with content designed to strengthen the employees' sense of being part of one big family. Some organisations began to set up works councils to channel communication down to ordinary employees. This process was carefully controlled. There was no opportunity for what we now call 'upward feedback'. Employees were told what the employers wanted them to know and, no doubt, made to feel grateful that they were being told anything at all.

So, was paternalism a good or a bad thing? Doubtless many employees benefited from a more caring attitude towards them. Equally, the whole system can be seen as one that demanded loyalty, unquestioning obedience to the rules and conformance to certain standards of behaviour in return for those benefits. Anyway, only a small proportion of the total workforce was able to enjoy these privileges. In many workplaces conditions could be positively Darwinian in the worst sense of the term. At the dockyards, for example, brass rods would be thrown into the crowd of unemployed men waiting outside the gates. Only those fit enough to fight off the others and get the rods back to the gate were hired.

---

8   Quoted in Robert Fitzgerald's *British Labour Management and Industrial Welfare 1846–1939* (Croom Helm, 1988), 10.
9   Lever Bros. and Cadbury built model villages at Port Sunlight and Bournville. Company housing was commonly provided in the shipbuilding, mining and railway industries.
10   For example *The Thames Ironworks Gazette* was launched in 1895. In the United States, when the first issue of *Western Electric News* appeared in 1912, it enthused that it was 'the answer to the universal demand of the employees for an opportunity to know more about this wonderful organisation'.

Workers as Dumb Animals

In 1915, a stonemason was busy engraving the words 'The Father of Scientific Management' on the tombstone of Frederick Winslow Taylor. This American mechanical engineer ushered in the next phase of industrial change by applying the new science of dynamics, the study of flows, to the way people carried out their tasks at work. His method was systematically to measure, analyse and then determine the ideal set of actions for any particular task that would increase productivity and reduce waste. Famous for using his stopwatch to measure the speed of specific actions, Taylor's new way of managing people sought to eliminate any vestiges of individual initiative.[11] A hundred years earlier, products had been standardised, now the actions of individual workers were to be standardised too.

Taylor cared little for the feelings of the workers. It's not certain that he saw them as human beings. He would regularly compare them to animals. Here's what he said about one particular job:

> *Now one of the very first requirements for a man who is fit to handle pig iron as a regular occupation is that he shall be so stupid and so phlegmatic that he more nearly resembles in his mental make-up the ox than any other type.*

When it came to communication, Taylor's approach was old-school:

> *Certain men are both thick-skinned and coarse-grained, and these individuals are apt to mistake a mild manner and a kindly way of saying things for timidity or weakness. With such men the severity both of words and manner should be gradually increased until either the desired result has been attained or the possibilities of the English language have been exhausted.*[12]

It's a shocking thought, but these attitudes are still around in many workplaces today. In any working environment where employees are given no discretion about how to do their work, there will be a tendency to drive them like pack animals.

---

11 Taylor's wasn't the only method of cutting costs and eliminating waste, there was also the Bedaux system. For more information see: www.internationalbedauxinstitute.com

12 From Frederick Winslow Taylor's *Shop Management* (1911 edition), quoted in Robert Kanigel, *The One Best Way* (Little Brown & Company, 1997), 354.

Workers as Machine Parts

Henry Ford saw the big picture. He understood that he needed customers to buy his vehicles, which meant helping to create a consumer society. He did his best to turn his workers into consumers, paying them five dollars a day, reducing daily working hours from nine to eight, and bringing in Saturday closing in his factories, helping to promote the idea of a 'weekend'. But to many eyes, as a result of the manufacturing methods he employed, men themselves had become mere extensions of the machine. Ford was in tune with many other managers of the time when he said: 'The average worker, I am sorry to say, wants a job in which he does not have to think'.

Ford's Detroit factory opened on 1 January 1910. It made use of machines designed to carry out specific tasks like moulding or drilling, replacing skilled labour. Workers were assigned to specific, repetitive tasks and the assembly line moved the materials to them in a never-ending stream of work. Machines set the pace. All unnecessary movements on the part of the worker were eliminated. The assembly line system produced incredible results from the manufacturer's point of view. Production increased in scale, prices dropped and the automobile market raced off. By 1920 half the cars in the world were Model T Fords.

Yet the workers were policed by Ford's security force, while his 'sociological department' kept tabs on their moral behaviour. They were urged to think of themselves as part of a successful company. The very first issue of *Ford Man*, the in-house magazine, without any sense of irony, exhorted the workers to see the factory as 'just as much yours as it is ours' – an early example of exhorting employees 'to take ownership'. For much of the twentieth century, employee communication like this was essentially propaganda.

Workers as Human Beings

By the 1920s, attitudes towards workers were beginning to change, very, very slowly but significantly. At the same time as scientific management was turning workers into machine parts, the new discipline of industrial psychology was becoming interested in measuring differences between individual employees. Methods of studying behaviour and mental testing, such as the IQ test, had been developed earlier in the century. People could now be classified in terms of intelligence and character.[13] It became evident that these new techniques could be helpful in areas like recruitment and job fit.

By 1923, Walter Dill Scott, one of the pioneers of what came to be known as the 'human relations movement', was able to say:

> *The personal differences between individuals have come to be recognised more and more as vital factors in industrial efficiency.*[14]

He pointed to the fact that, as he saw it, in most organisations workers had become commodities, bought at the lowest price in the market. He felt that many employers treated their people as 'mere operating mechanisms'. He dedicated a significant part of his book on personnel management to descriptions of test methods for individual attributes such as muscular strength, mental alertness, memory and perception, imagination and emotion, reaction times, even vocational interests.

Much of his argument was far-sighted and well ahead of its time. For example, he suggested that workers could be seen as citizens with the right 'of having a voice in determining the rules and regulations under which they work'. He urged managers to think of employees as 'customers' who 'know more about the detailed operation of the industry than the owner or manager'. He felt that 'the company should sell itself to the employee' by providing information, including on such matters as the 'social and moral environment' and 'worthwhileness of the company's product'. It took another 50 years or so for ideas like this to percolate into employee communication.

Meanwhile, other industrial psychologists were busy exploring this curious phenomenon called 'workers'. What was going on in their minds, if anything? What would get them to work harder? In 1924 an experiment began in the Hawthorne Works of the Western Electric Company in the United States. The original intention of the study was to see if better lighting in the factory led to increased productivity. Researchers found that productivity increased both when the lighting was improved and when it was made worse. Further tests had similar results even when other variables were added in such as group incentives, rest periods, reduced working hours and free lunches.

---

13 During the First World War nearly two million recruits into the American Army were given intelligence tests. Psychologist Robert Yerkes and his team developed tests that could be administered to large groups. This new technique of measurement gave psychology a scientific basis for the investigation of differences between individuals.

14 All quotations of Walter Dill Scott are from his book *Personnel Management* (McGraw-Hill, 1923), vii, 3–12, 310.

It began to dawn on the researchers that ordinary working people were actually quite complex beings who did not respond predictably to particular stimuli. To try and get behind the mysterious results, more than 21,000 employees were interviewed between 1928 and 1930. In due course, the research team came to, what might seem to us, a blindingly obvious conclusion – namely that people are different, so different that what acts as an incentive for one person may be a disincentive for another. They also discovered that workers' behaviour was heavily influenced by what was happening to the group as a whole, as well as by relationships between individuals.

Although the Hawthorne studies have been heavily criticised from both technical and ethical standpoints, they prodded psychologists into finding better ways of measuring and analysing how workers' attitudes affected their behaviour. The tools for this were becoming available. In 1928 Louis Thurstone published *Attitudes Can Be Measured*. By using multiple-factor analysis he set out to give attitude measurement a robust mathematical foundation. His hope was that he had developed 'tools by which to reduce the complexities of social and psychological phenomena to a limited number of elements'.[15]

In fact, Thurstone's method became less popular than Rensis Likert's, which is much simpler. In 1932 Likert published *A Technique for the Measurement of Attitudes*, which uses a five-point scale (sometimes also seven or nine points) to denote agreement or disagreement with a statement. This is the type of scale still in common use today which ranges from, say, 'strongly agree' to 'strongly disagree' with a neutral response in the middle.

The building blocks of future employee communication were piling up by the 1930s. Yet employee attitude surveys didn't become commonplace until the 1990s. In 1937, the headline in the house magazine of big American advertising agency J. Walter Thompson made an astonishing announcement. It declared: 'Workers are people!'[16]

Workers Need to be Motivated

Once psychologists had realised that human beings were complex individuals, the floodgates opened and motivational theories poured out. 'What do people want?' 'How can we get them to do what we want them to do freely and willingly?' It was becoming clear that the best way of controlling employees was

---

15   Louis Leon Thurstone, *The Vectors of Mind: Multiple-Factor Analysis for the Isolation of Primary Traits* (University of Chicago Press, 1935).
16   Roland Marchand, *Creating the Corporate Soul* (University of California Press, 1998), 214.

to get inside their minds. Of all the motivational theories that emerged after the Second World War two stand out in particular.

Abraham Maslow first published a paper on 'A Theory of Motivation' in 1943 in which he said:

> *Man is a wanting animal and rarely reaches a state of complete satisfaction except for a short time. As one desire is satisfied, another pops up to take its place.*

He went on to construct a 'Model of Human Needs' which is usually shown as a pyramid. At the base of the pyramid are the basic 'physiological' needs, all those things we need to do to survive, like eating and sleeping. Once the basic needs are satisfied the human wants to be safe, and only once that's achieved can social relations become a source of satisfaction. The social human then looks for self-esteem and finally self-actualisation. At the very tip of the pyramid are all the higher order needs that make humans feel they are living life as fully as it can be lived.

Picking up on Maslow's ideas, Professor Douglas McGregor published *The Human Side of Enterprise* in 1960 and made the point that the attitude managers took towards the people they managed made all the difference to the way they dealt with them. He described two alternative ways of thinking about working people and called them Theory X and Theory Y. He said if you are a Theory X manager you are likely to believe that most people inherently dislike work and will avoid it if they can. This means you need a strict system of direction, command and control. If you are a Theory Y manager you are convinced that employees will work hard and effectively if their goals are the same as those of the organisation. The individual will self-direct and take full personal responsibility for achieving the objectives. Today, although there are still plenty of Theory X managers about, Theory Y has evolved into the predominant model for encouraging higher performance, and is at the heart of contemporary employee communication.

All this represented a sea-change in attitudes towards managing people. By the late 1950s it was acceptable to show contempt for what were now seen as the 'old-fashioned' methods of scientific management. More advanced theories on the way to manage and motivate people began to appear, advocating techniques such as goal setting and job enrichment. More emphasis was put on the importance of trust and fairness in the workplace and good communication.

Them and Us

In broad terms, it's true to say that until the 1950s, the tug-of-war between employers, power from above, and workers, power from below, had been an unequal match. Despite a lot of strikes and disruption, more powerful forces were lined up on the employers' side. But then, during the so-called 'golden age' after the Second World War, in conditions of full employment, trade unions sought to make rapid progress towards the improvement of pay, working conditions, job security and benefits for their members.

This period in Britain was characterised by a mixture of complacency and incompetence on the part of management, and frustrated aggression on the part of unionised workers. The problem was cultural. A deeply embedded class system, attitudes of superiority and even racism towards foreign competitors, a refusal to consider modern 'American' methods of management, led to declining industries. The workforce was still seen as a class apart by senior managers who:

> just sat in their offices 'making policy', lunching at the Savoy, going to trade associations, overseas tours, heaven knows what, but doing little we could recognise as work.[17]

Meanwhile, unions dominated the channels of communication to workers, and senior managers were content to let it be so. This was an era of collaboration and 'consensus' when it was felt necessary to avoid confrontation as much as possible, despite 'power from below' often taking the form of strikes and other conflicts. Managers turned a blind eye towards the growth of restrictive practices that included 'closed shops' (where only members of a particular union could work), restrictions on the employment of women and limitations on machine manning and output. The 'collective voice' of workers became synonymous with the opinions of the leading trade unions or, in some cases, local union shop stewards.

This was the time when the 'them and us' culture was at its worst, though it still exists in some workplaces today. Society was riddled with class distinctions and social snobbery. Many managers, including senior ones, were unqualified and dismissive of education, preferring people to learn 'on the job'. The vast majority of workers were still receiving a minimal level of education. Memories

---

17 David Kynaston, *Modernity Britain: A Shake of the Dice 1959–62* (Bloomsbury, 2014), 142, quoting Lord (Arnold) Weinstock.

of the 1930s depression, unemployment and hardship remained fresh in their minds.

This was also the era of central planning, 'power from above' in a pure form. Plans formulated by an elite in HQ would be sent out to the divisions. Following an almost military approach, orders would cascade down through layers of management to be carried out by the front-line 'troops'. The concept of 'management by objectives' took hold. In an environment like this, there was no need to think very deeply about employee communication. As a result, from the 1950s to the 1970s, most of the communication from management to employees was a form of internal public relations, carried out through the medium of house publications.

Internal PR

The business discipline of 'internal communications' began to emerge as a more professional entity just after the Second World War. For example, the British Association of Industrial Editors (BAIE) held its first meeting in 1949. Its aim was to create a professional organisation to support 'the amorphous mass of journalists, advertising men, company secretaries' secretaries, welfare offices, publicity men, sports club managers'[18] who were responsible for publishing house journals. By 1959 BAIE reported a total circulation of 4.3 million employees for the publications produced by its 503 member companies.[19] By the 1970s this figure had grown to around 2,000[20] internal newspapers and magazines.

Some of these magazines might be seen as remnants of the paternalism of former times, stuffed as they were with social stories about employees' births, deaths, marriages and sports events. Others were more focused on the organisation itself, featuring Q&A sessions with chief executives as well as readers' letters. A number of companies produced special reports for employees simplifying financial results and other business issues. In response to this growing market, specialist house journal agencies formed, employing journalists who had worked in the national press.

---

18 Steve Knight and David Knight, *The Rise and Rise of Internal Communication* (British Association of Communicators in Business, 2009), 8.
19 By way of comparison, by 1950 in the United States, there were 6,500 in-house publications distributed to around 80 million employees.
20 Figure sourced from two 1978 reports by Business Decisions Ltd and Oyez Intelligence.

However, there were still many senior managers who saw employee communication, if they thought about it at all, as just a subset of the personnel department's activities, and certainly not a strategic issue for them to spend time on. Even if they had an internal publication, the vast majority of organisations in the 1970s had no formal employee communications policy, strategy or even a thought-out plan with clear objectives. The rather vague approach of the time is summed up by one respondent who, in a Business Decisions survey of 1978, said that employee communication is 'a public relations exercise. If you have any faith in public relations you must see the value of it'.

Internal Marketing

When the concept of 'internal marketing' arrived on the scene in the 1980s, it finally brought to life Dill Scott's idea, expressed back in 1923, that 'the company should sell itself to the employee'. It was the beginning of a concerted attempt to use persuasive communication to motivate employees.

The turn from internal PR to internal marketing took place in the context of a growing awareness of the need for companies to improve their standards of service and the quality of their products. Ideas the Japanese had adopted years before began to filter into Western organisations. Concepts like Total Quality Management, with its emphasis on 'the consumer being the most important part of the production line', made it important to encourage 'pride of workmanship'.[21] Internal marketing came to be seen as the way to increase employees' awareness of the need for higher standards across a range of work activities.

A new terminology appeared. Organisations started to talk about using communication to 'align' their employees with organisational goals, especially quality and customer service. 'Vision' and 'Mission' statements became all the rage. Employees were given little vision and mission cards to stick in their top pockets or handbags. The idea that different departments should treat each other as 'internal customers' became popular in some organisations.

By the 1990s these ideas had built up a head of steam. Extra momentum came as the balance of the economy swung away from manufacturing towards service industries. The appearance of desktop computers undermined hierarchical systems of command and control.[22] Layers of management were

---

21   For a full discussion of this subject see Henry R. Neave, *The Deming Dimension* (SPC Press, 1990).

22   Although the first personal computer was offered for sale in 1977, it took around another 25 years for desktop computers to become widespread.

cut back. It became important to persuade individual employees that they were trusted to be more autonomous and make more decisions.

The buzzword 'empowerment' appeared. It was used by managers as shorthand for suggesting that employees could take more responsibility and make more decisions, though surveys revealed that many employees saw it as a way for the organisation to get more work out of people for the same money. Yet the use of the word 'empowerment' signalled an important strategic shift. The tectonic plates of management theory were grinding up against each other and throwing up new ways of looking at the workforce. The 'old theories' based on Taylorism, Fordism and top-down planning were coming up against arguments that emphasised the need for organisations to be much more flexible and adaptive. 'Strategy' needed to be the practical response to changing conditions rather than a fixed, dogmatic set of concepts.

This placed a new emphasis on employees as a source of competitive advantage. Somehow, organisations needed to begin to tap into the ideas and knowledge of individual employees. Managers talked about giving employees greater 'autonomy'. Autonomy was never clearly defined, but reflected the need to give employees more freedom in how they carried out their work. There was a fashion for creating 'learning organisations'.

Employee attitude surveys proliferated as managements sought to measure their internal culture. People began to talk less about 'management' and more about 'leadership'. More and more new language appeared in the workplace where, far from being 'workers', some employees were now being called 'colleagues', 'partners' or 'associates'. Everybody was expected to be 'passionate' about what they were doing.

Yet at the same time, 'power from above' maintained its grip and took the form of new metrics such as Balanced Score Cards, Key Performance Indicators and Dashboards. Tightly focused concepts like the primacy of 'maximising shareholder value' were promoted. A wave of Business Process Re-Engineering swept through organisations, leaving fear and insecurity in its wake.

Getting Engaged

From the 1990s onwards, more and more internal communication specialists were being recruited. In 2014, a report appeared suggesting that around 45,000 people in the UK were in a role that encompassed employee communications.[23]

---

23 *Size of the Sector* (Institute of Internal Communication, 2014), 7.

All this activity was centred on one central, strategic question posed by senior managers – 'how can we motivate our employees to achieve a higher level of performance in those areas which we deem crucial to the organisation's success?' That this question was being asked was an acknowledgement that the success of organisations was now less a question of brilliant leadership, than being able to persuade employees to 'give of their best'.

As the new millennium approached, employee communications was finally beginning to be recognised as a vital component in organisational strategy - no longer a 'nice to have' but a 'must have'. The emphasis, though, was still on getting employees to 'perform'. Although managers were starting to talk about employee 'well-being', the view from the top remained firmly that what really mattered was the drive to reduce costs and increase productivity. 'Work smarter not harder', some leaders urged. But it became obvious that, in the era of desktop computers and mobile communications technology, people would have to work both smarter and harder.

By the first decade of the twenty-first century, the employee communication role had expanded enormously. It had become strategic. A new orthodoxy sprang up. The vast majority of senior managers were likely to agree that employee motivation was key to their organisation's success. Their aim became to win over the hearts and minds of employees to the values and goals of the organisation. Another buzzword has come along to describe this state of affairs – 'engagement'.

An 'engaged employee' is the employer's ideal worker – committed, caring about doing a good job, emotionally attached to the work in some way, taking responsibility, collaborating with others, going the extra mile and so on.

But as with all these fashionable, management-speak words, there's a problem. First, there appear to be many different definitions of what being 'engaged' really means. Second, the word is a metaphorical throwback to the age of machines. Perhaps it's subliminal, but by asking employees to become 'engaged' senior managers are in danger of thinking of them as cogs and gears in the great organisational machine, just like their nineteenth and twentieth-century predecessors. Third, 'engagement' is not a word that emerges naturally from the mouths of employees themselves.

In any case, communication aimed at getting employees engaged doesn't appear to be working. Research in Britain shows that in the highest scoring organisations just 24 per cent of employees are 'highly engaged'; in the lowest scoring it was just 3 per cent.[24] A 2013 worldwide Gallup poll was even

---

24   David MacLeod and Nita Clarke, *Engaging for Success: Enhancing Performance through Employee Engagement*, a report to government (2009), 15.

gloomier, showing just 13 per cent of employees worldwide are 'engaged'.[25] It's not surprising. Employees know that a lot of the communication aimed at them is designed to motivate them to perform – to produce more for less. In a world where employees are becoming increasingly educated and worldly-wise this type of Motivational Communication just won't do any more. It's time to take a different approach.

Principled Persuasion

Take a step back. Ask yourself what the aim of employee communication should be in the twenty-first century. Does it make sense to continue down the path of Motivational Communication, with its faithful attendants, indoctrination and neo-paternalism, never far away? My answer is that it doesn't make any sense at all, except to organisations that want to have an 'engineered workplace', valuing employees only for the work they can get out of them.

Instead, the time has come to rethink the role of the employee communications professional. In the next few decades, as I'll explain in the next chapter, there are going to be profound changes in the world of work. Communication within organisations is going to become far more important than it is now. Switching from Motivational Communication to Principled Persuasion is the way forward. That's because the aim of Principled Persuasion is not to control employees from within their own minds – on the contrary, its primary goal is to liberate them from the stifling constraints that so many organisations continue to impose on them.

The agenda for Principled Persuaders is to use persuasive communication to create happier, less harmful, more ethical working environments in which employees can flourish as individuals. This will be achieved by using language that is clearer, more meaningful, more rhetorically powerful and more truthful. Principled Persuaders will move into the centre of the organisation as the strategic importance of internal communication is fully recognised. Principled Persuasion will resolve the tension between 'power from above' and 'power from below'.

As a business discipline, Principled Persuasion will become a focal point around which a whole new range of communication channels and analytics can

---

25 Gallup, *The State of the Global Workplace: Employee Engagement Insights for Business Leaders Worldwide* (2013), 11.

be built. This is going to be an essential development for organisations if they are to survive and prosper in a continuously changing world. Why this is the case is the subject of the next chapter.

CHAPTER 2

Pathways to the Future: Five Converging Forces Shaping the Future of Work

When Bill Clinton assembled the top minds of the nation to discuss the economy in 1992, no one mentioned the internet.[1]

No one can predict the future. What we can do is examine the forces that, right now, look most likely to carve out the future of work. I'm going to focus on five of them. Each one is immensely powerful in its own right. Together they are going to transform the world of work forever.

I'm calling them the 'Five Converging Forces'. They are:

- information;
- automation;
- education;
- mentalisation;
- communication.

The convergence of these Five Converging Forces will pose immense ethical and logistical challenges for organisations. As you will see, they will present organisational leaders with a choice of two pathways to the future, going in entirely different directions.

One pathway will continue on the same track that, since the nineteenth century, has led organisations to exert more and more control over their employees. In these workplaces, 'Motivational Communication' is deployed to bring employees into alignment with the organisation's values and culture. New technologies are used for constant surveillance, monitoring and

---

1   Erik Brynjolfsson and Andrew McAfee, *Race Against the Machine* (Digital Frontier Press, 2011), 74.

increasing the pressure of work. This is the ENGINEERED ORGANISATION, where the management mindset of the nineteenth and twentieth centuries continues. Employees are seen as well-greased cogs and gears fitting into established processes and systems.

The other pathway heads towards a new type of working environment. Here the emphasis is on freeing up employees to flourish as individuals. Fostered by Principled Persuasion, the culture will be one of freedom of communication and movement. This will make work more pleasurable, as well as stimulating innovation and creative thinking in all parts of the organisation. This is the PROGRESSIVE ORGANISATION where managers have a twenty-first-century mindset, where new technologies are used to create a rich and fertile ecosystem – a new type of organisational culture.

In the ENGINEERED ORGANISATION employees will continue to be 'human resources'. In the PROGRESSIVE ORGANISATION they will be seen as 'resourceful humans'.

The Five Converging Forces

These five powerful forces haven't arrived from nowhere. All of them are continuations of trends that have been around for a very long time. They are like supertankers that have been slowly gathering speed and are now building up a tremendous momentum. As they surge forward they push out enormous bow waves that threaten to sink the unwary.

So let's get to it, starting with INFORMATION.

INFORMATION

For knowledge itself is power.[2]

In Roman times, information travelled at an average speed of 1 mile per hour.[3] And there wasn't much information anyway. The invention of the printing press in around 1450 AD gave information its first massive boost. In the 50 years between 1453 and 1503 around eight million books were printed, more

---

2   Attributed to Francis Bacon. The original phrase was 'ipsa scientia potestas est' from *Meditationes Sacrae* [*Religious Meditations*] (1597)·

3   Estimate from Gregory Clark, *A Farewell to Alms* (Princeton University Press, 2007), 305–6·

than all the scribes of Europe had produced in the previous 1,200 years. It's estimated that around 130 million unique books have been printed in total up to now.[4] But that's nothing compared to what's coming. According to experts,[5] every two years we are creating as much information as was gathered since the dawn of civilisation.

A mountain of information looms over us all – much of it instantly accessible through the Internet. Yet, we are still only on the threshold of the information revolution. We are about to witness a huge increase in computer power, together with a rapid spread of intelligent sensors.

Do you know the story of the second half of the chessboard? Here's a short version. A chessboard has 64 squares, so 32 in each half. Put one grain of rice on the first square. Then put two on the next square, and keep doubling the number of grains until you've used each square on the first half of the chessboard. By the 32nd square you will have needed four billion grains of rice. Keep going onto the second half and by the end you'll need a pile of rice as big as Mount Everest.[6]

Now let's think about computer power. Between the late 1950s and 2006 there were around 32 doublings. 'Moore's Law',[7] which predicted a doubling of computer power every year to 18 months, had been proved correct. By some estimates there has been a 137 billionfold increase in computer power in the last half-century.[8] So now we're already on the second half of the chessboard.

This massive increase in computer power means new algorithms can be created to turn information into knowledge. Unlike humans, algorithms can keep masses of data in working memory – and they're not affected by distractions or moods. So they are able to spot things that would never occur to a human being. They can identify patterns and links that were previously undiscoverable.

This is the world of 'Big Data'. And Big Data can be used to create Big Brother organisations. Linked to sensors that track movements, powerful computers using Big Data techniques will enable managers to indulge in what some have called 'reality mining'.

---

4   Viktor Mayer-Schonberger and Kenneth Cukier, *Big Data* (John Murray, 2013), 84.
5   Eric Schmidt and Jared Cohen, *The New Digital Age* (John Murray, 2013), 253.
6   That's $2^{64}-1$ grains of rice. Brynjolfsson and McAfee, *Race Against the Machine*, 19.
7   In 1965 Gordon E. Moore, the 36-year-old director of Fairchild's Research and Development Laboratories, observed that the complexity of 'minimum cost semiconductor components' had been doubling once a year every year since the first prototype microchip had been produced five years before. He claimed that this doubling would continue every year for the next ten years. Carver Mead, a professor at Caltech, called this 'Moore's Law'. It evolved into the prediction that the power of information technology will continue to double every 18 months.
8   Stewart Brand, *The Clock of the Long Now* (Weidenfeld & Nicolson, 1999), 13.

Imagine this. Every employee is obliged to wear a smart sensor embedded in work clothes or a security pass. The sensor feeds information in real time about every movement the employee makes. In due course, the millions of bits of information on employee movements can be used for different purposes. One might be to establish patterns of behaviour at work: how long do people spend at their desks or wandering around? How much time is spent on the telephone or computer? Another might be to track links between different parts of the organisation. Who is meeting whom? And for how long? Management in general can use the data to push for efficiency improvements; HR departments might well use data on individuals to inform their performance assessments.

If this seems a little far-fetched, it's worth noting that 'technologies of intrusion' already exist. There's even a new word for it – 'dataveillance'. Cameras are everywhere. Many organisations already monitor their employees' use of computers by tracking keystrokes, checking what's on their screens, recording their Internet use and screening emails.

But this kind of information technology can be used in a different way. In the PROGRESSIVE ORGANISATION, enlightened managers will use these new, powerful technologies of data gathering and analysis to share insights and knowledge with all employees. Their objective will be to enrich employees' working experience, not impoverish it.

Patterns of behaviour will still be analysed, but this time instead of being used to create more rules and regulations, the information can be shared and discussed in order to see what insights the employees can have themselves on the way people work. Information on the degrees of contact between different parts of the organisation can be used to highlight those areas where more contact would be beneficial.

Software will be incorporated into employees' computers and smartphones to give them access to the organisation's database. The information each employee receives can be tailored according to the tasks they are working on at the time. This is where algorithms can come into play. For example, online booksellers use algorithms to suggest titles you might like, based on links between what you and others have ordered. New information systems might weigh up the task an employee is working on and then suggest contact with a certain person, or reading some specific material in order to round out knowledge in a particular area.

This type of 'knowledge management' in organisations could become a highly sophisticated process. It would encourage individuals to make personal connections, take an online course, brush up on a specific topic – all with the aim of not only moving the task or project forward, but also helping the individual employee grow in knowledge and experience.

Meanwhile, in contrast to the Motivational Communicator who will be busy promoting the importance of using specified information to increase efficiency, the Principled Persuader will work with ICT experts to create a 'knowledge map' of the organisation, and share this with employees.

The aim will be to create a culture in which employees can go looking for more relevant information with guidance from the knowledge map. After all, if you don't know about something, it is difficult to conceive that it exists. The powerful information systems of the future, in PROGRESSIVE ORGANISATIONS, will bring to employees' attention knowledge they might otherwise have missed out on.

AUTOMATION

The vastly increasing power of computers, the arrival of intelligent sensors, the analytics of Big Data and access to information in the cloud create a perfect breeding ground for automation and robots of all kinds. Indeed, the impending robot revolution will change the nature of working life and the shape of organisations. Many new jobs will be created and many destroyed.

The tide of automation has been rising steadily for two centuries. We now take it for granted and often hardly even notice the changes taking place. But the rate at which machines replace human activity is about to accelerate rapidly.

Some experts[9] think this will lead to widespread job destruction – that almost half the job roles currently occupied by humans will be taken over by robots. They believe that:

> *most workers in transport and logistics operations, together with the bulk of office and administration support workers and labour in production operations are at risk.*

Many thousands of little robots are already busy cleaning people's houses; some hospitals are using 'trundlebots' that move trolleys around the building; armed services deploy aerial drones extensively for reconnaissance and killing

---

9   Carl Benedikt Frey and Michael A. Osborne, *The Future of Employment: How Susceptible are Jobs to Computerisation?* (September 2013), 44.

specified targets; the car and electronic industries have been investing in industrial robots for some time and are set to invest in them even more heavily.[10]

The potential for robots to take over dull, dangerous and dirty jobs is huge. The disaster at Japan's Fukushima Daiichi nuclear power plant in 2011 highlighted the need for emergency robots to wade into life-threatening situations instead of people. Pipelines and pylons, difficult to access, will be serviced and cleaned by robots rather than technicians. Drones will be used to monitor crops across large areas of farmland. A four-wheeled robot, the driverless car, is on its way.

The list of possibilities for commercial and industrial robots seems almost endless. But robots can be cute and cuddly too. There is a big role for them in the caring services. They can be used to medically monitor the elderly and infirm, sending real-time data back to care providers. Robot pets are already being used to help some dementia patients.

The arrival of smart sensors will enable robot to talk to robot, machine to machine. It is estimated[11] that by 2030 there may be as many as one trillion embedded devices talking to each other through the Internet.

New opportunities for jobs, new threats. Robots won't just replace low-skilled workers working on routine and repetitive tasks, but some 'knowledge workers' too: experts believe that 'sophisticated algorithms could substitute for approximately 140 million full-time knowledge workers worldwide'.[12] For example, in the health arena, surgical robots are already at work and the near future should see robots capable of diagnosis, with access to unimaginably more data than even the most experienced specialist. Scanners, linked to powerful computers, are already being used instead of lawyers to pick out important data from legal documents.

The rapid and successful introduction of robots is going to become a key source of competitive advantage between nations. New geographic realignments of manufacturing and assembly plants will take place as organisations cease to chase low-cost human labour around the world and use robots at home instead.

The pace at which all this will happen depends on the willingness of organisations to invest in automata. As more robots are used, costs will drop and more organisations will find it viable to invest. But whatever the exact timing, the effect of robots on the workplace is going to be significant in

---

10 Taiwanese company, Foxconn, with around 1.2 million employees on its assembly lines, has brought in thousands of robots to build the Apple iPhone 6.
11 Adjiedj Bakas, *Megatrends Europe: The Future of a Continent* (Marshall Cavendish, 2006).
12 Frey and Osborne, 'The Future of Employment', 19.

two main ways; many jobs will be lost and new jobs will be created – in what proportions, no one knows.

ENGINEERED ORGANISATIONS will use robots to replace human workers, increase efficiency, lower costs and boost profit. But even those organisations will need to create new jobs[13] to run and maintain their robot army. However, PROGRESSIVE ORGANISATIONS will see the advancing waves of robots as an opportunity to take humans off routine, repetitive, 'screen-sitting' tasks and free them to use their unique capabilities in providing services to other human beings. Robots won't be able to compete with humans on empathy and creativity for many years to come.

A reduction in routine work for human beings should be seen as a mark of social progress. The transition to a robot-rich working environment will entail a change of mindset on the part of all employees, especially senior managers. Human labour will be channelled into concentrating on activities only humans can engage in. That means more time dedicated to thinking, discussing, planning, innovating and person-to-person interactions.

But how is this transition to be accomplished? How is it going to be possible for employees accustomed to routine work, to switch into carrying out more complex tasks involving thought and judgement and social skills? That's where the third strategic driver of change comes in – education. There will need to be a continuous process of re-skilling on a massive scale. The PROGRESSIVE ORGANISATION will create an environment where education is an intrinsic part of normal working life.

EDUCATION

If you think education is expensive, try ignorance.[14]

The strategic power of education should never be underestimated. Humanity's survival and prosperity depends on it.

Everyone nowadays at least pays lip service to the importance of education. But it was not always so. Throughout the nineteenth century and into the twentieth large sections of the ruling classes did not look favourably on the

---

13   In a recent report (Peter Gorle and Andrew Clive, *Positive Impact of Industrial Robots on Employment* (International Federation of Robotics, 2013), 8–10), it is claimed that over 500,000 jobs were created worldwide due to robotics in 2008–11, and that the potential for new jobs between 2012 and 2016 is up to 1.5 million, and in 2017–20, 1–2 million.

14   Attributed to Derek Bok, an American academic (1978).

idea of educating the working class. After all, education spreads ideas that can challenge the establishment.

The fierce demand we see for education around the world is something quite new. At the moment, understandably, the focus is on educating the young. But this is already changing, at least in advanced societies, where the concept of 'lifelong learning' is entrenching itself. This is a response both to the fact of increased longevity, and to the rapidly changing artistic, scientific and technological environment. People now want to learn more for longer. Yet the provision for learning in the workplace is very limited for most people.

That's because opportunities for education have evolved very slowly, and we are only just now at the beginning of what promises to be a massive upsurge in demand for education. Take Great Britain, the birthplace of the Industrial Revolution, for example.

As we saw in Chapter 1, by the end of the nineteenth century steps were being taken to provide some basic education to the working poor. In England, by the 1870s, school boards had begun educating some children up to the age of ten. But school-leaving ages crept up slowly: to 14 by 1918, 15 by 1947, 16 by 1972. It's only by 2015 that everyone in Britain under the age of eighteen should be in some form of education or training.

As for universities, just 1.5 per cent of 18-year-olds in Britain enjoyed higher education in the 1920s. By the 1950s the figure had risen to just 2 per cent. It was only in the 1960s that universities began to expand. Now Britain has reached the point where there are half a million university places available each year, allowing around 50 per cent of 18-year-olds to go on to higher studies.

Different countries have followed different educational trajectories from Britain but the general point remains valid; the educational revolution has only just started. The next few decades will see a huge expansion in the numbers of people being educated worldwide. New technologies will make access to education easier, such as machine algorithms embodied in online programmes designed to meet an individual student's needs.

However, there is a problem. The current job market lags behind in providing stimulating jobs that make the best use of people's skills and knowledge. Yet many young people are being over-educated – the quality of jobs just can't keep up with the quality of education. Already, back in 1973, commentators were complaining: 'we have sought to employ educated workers in old types of routine work'.[15] More recently, in 2011, a leading educationalist[16] concluded:

---

15   Fred Best, *The Future of Work* (Prentice Hall, 1973), 101.
16   Alison Wolf, *Review of Vocational Education: The Wolf Report* (2011), 35.

'The UK workforce, in aggregate, already possesses far more qualifications at a given, overall level, than most occupations require'.

In the UK it's estimated up to a third of younger employees are overqualified for the work they are doing;[17] 52 per cent of employees rate their skills as higher than needed to do their jobs;[18] 63 per cent of part-time workers are working at levels below their skills and qualifications.[19]

It's the same story the world over.

The net effect has been termed 'educational inflation'. University graduates are now taking jobs that used to be taken by school leavers. That pushes school leavers into lower skilled jobs and unskilled people out of the jobs market altogether. Given that it's estimated only around a third of all jobs constitute 'knowledge working', that leaves a lot of people looking for jobs that match their skills and qualifications.

This problem will get worse as automata take on more of the workload and organisations struggle to find enough interesting and stretching roles for their increasingly well-educated staff. This is a recipe for serious dissatisfaction at work. New thinking is required.

That's where the PROGRESSIVE ORGANISATION comes in. Leaders here will believe that entering the workplace represents not the end of education, but the beginning of a lifelong learning experience.

The ENGINEERED ORGANISATION will stick to providing the minimum of training necessary to plug skills gaps and enhance knowledge in specifically targeted areas. The PROGRESSIVE ORGANISATION will embrace the concept that great progress can be made from the cumulative effect of hundreds of individual ideas, jostling together in interconnected networks, stimulated by continuous education and training.

The PROGRESSIVE ORGANISATION will foster a culture of sharing ideas, challenging outmoded ways of thinking and looking for innovative ways of providing goods and services. It will understand that education is an investment, not a cost, and that education has a fundamental strategic role in opening minds and creating new perspectives – mental processes that are at the heart of innovation and creativity.

The demand is there. The Equal Opportunities Commission reported:

---

17 Wolf, *Review of Vocational Education*, 29.
18 Brigid van Wanrooy, Helen Bewley, Alex Bryson, John Forth, Stephanie Freeth, Lucy Stokes and Stephen Wood, *The 2011 Workplace Employment Relations Study*, 37.
19 Katie Holmes, *The Future of Work: Individuals and Workplace Transformation* (Equal Opportunities Commission, 2007), ix.

> *Many [employees] ... appreciate the time and resources to continually
> develop themselves, improving their craft or learning new skills, with
> a positive attitude to lifelong learning.*[20]

But will the supply be there?

There is an urgent need to begin creating new educational infrastructures for employees, based on a combination of what the organisation needs in terms of knowledge and skills, and what the employees themselves wish to learn about. In the PROGRESSIVE ORGANISATION, Principled Persuaders will be active in working with experts to design new educational opportunities for employees. They'll use research to find out what's needed, and tap into a new industry of occupational education providers.

The alternative is grim. Without the stimulus of further learning opportunities, well-educated employees will become increasingly dissatisfied with life at work. Productivity will suffer – economic and social progress will slow down.

MENTALISATION

So, what is 'mentalisation'? It's a term that encompasses the whole process of trying to understand mental states, ours and other people's. Such understanding can be used to control ourselves and others. It's an age-old quest that's been particularly active since psychology sprang into life as a science in the 1870s. Ever since then there has been a determined attempt to understand the 'mechanisms' through which the mind works and find ways of adjusting them to alter thoughts and behaviour.

In Chapter 1 we saw the impact that the psychology of motivation had on organisations. In the late twentieth century, Motivational Communication developed as a tool of management, designed to get employees to 'buy into' mission and values and to work harder as a result. In the twenty-first century, the endless flow of psychological experiments, and detailed exploration of the brain's physics and chemistry by neuroscientists, will provide more techniques for the measurement and influencing of minds.

Such techniques are already in use in 'neuromarketing'. Measuring electrical signals in the brain through EEG sensors, or more rarely full-on brain scans, neuromarketeers aim to 'reach consumers minds at the preconscious,

---

20 Holmes, *The Future of Work*, 20.

precognitive level, where responses are unbiased and unfiltered'.[21] It's not a big jump to imagine a future where measurement of brain activity and structure is used in recruitment and selection of people for promotion. Managers will be able to tell whether candidates really believe in the organisation's values or they're just saying they do!

As neuroscientists continue to explore the chemistry and physics of the brain, they will discover more and more links between brain structure and behaviour. This could lead to a system of screening and filtering to ensure the perfect 'fit' of an individual to a position. For example, an individual's creative potential might be assessed by measuring the degree of symmetry between the temporo-parietal lobes.[22] As neuroscientists compile ever larger databases on brain activity and structure, 'neurometrics' will emerge to take over from psychometrics and other forms of character tests.

It's also likely that the future will bring a sharp increase in the use of 'psychotropic' drugs – that is drugs designed to alter the mind in one way or another. They are already commonly used. Caffeine, cocaine, amphetamine and ecstasy stimulate the mind. Alcohol, morphine and cannabis are depressants. You can take Prozac to remedy depression, Ritalin to help you pay attention, Paxil to make you less shy, Sarafem to make you less moody, steroids for boosting your physical strength and Librium to give you 'equilibrium'. Modafinil keeps soldiers and pilots awake for days.

Most organisations have absolutely no idea what drugs their employees are taking. Nor do many senior managers concern themselves over the mental health of their employees (see page 78). But it's easy to see how the use of performance-enhancing psychotropic drugs could become part of an organisational culture, officially or unofficially. The fact is that many people at work are already using mind-altering drugs, some legally, some illegally. The 'transhumanist'[23] movement predicts that drugs will be used by some organisations, not just the military, to help people boost their memory, supercharge their ability to work with complex mathematics, or learn a new language.

It's not hard to see how hard-pressed, highly competitive organisations might start to introduce the use of psychotropic drugs as a way of enhancing organisational performance, particularly with employees engaged in critical activities. Once genetic screening has advanced enough, it might even be possible to tailor medications to individuals.

---

21 A.K. Pradeep, *The Buying Brain* (Wiley, 2010), quotation from the inside cover blurb.
22 Susan Greenfield, *The Quest for Identity in the 21st Century* (Sceptre, 2008), 253–75.
23 Joel Garreau, *Radical Evolution* (Doubleday, 2005), 227–65.

If we're not careful, it won't be very long before ENGINEERED ORGANISATIONS start to have their own 'behavioural management' teams using psychological and 'neuromanagement' techniques to exercise even greater control over employees. The convergence of psychology with neuroscience promises to offer many new opportunities for getting inside people's minds and influencing their beliefs and behaviour.

There's no way of stopping the advance in knowledge of how the human brain works. It's how we use that knowledge that matters.

The PROGRESSIVE ORGANISATION, instead of seeking to control employees, will set out to open up this whole area for debate and discussion. For example, one of the first things it can do is remove the taboo on talking about mental health issues at work. It will set out to measure the mental health of the organisation's employees and work out ways of providing help to those who need it. It will have a clear ethical code for the use of legal drugs in the working environment.

What's more, with the help of Principled Persuaders, the PROGRESSIVE ORGANISATION will educate employees on the basic principles of psychology. Since the development of the Neuro-Linguistic Programming (NLP) movement in the 1970s, there have been attempts to widen the consciousness of people at work. NLP practitioners help individuals to understand more about the neurological system and how to use language effectively. But NLP reached very few employees. The time is fast arriving when all employees will benefit from a greater understanding of how the mind works. To avoid the situation where those with greater mentalisation skills exert power over those without them, the discipline of Principled Persuasion will need to work hard within organisations to democratise knowledge of psychology and the workings of the brain.

COMMUNICATION

When are senior managers in organisations going to take the subject of internal communication seriously? Yes I know there have been great advances in recent decades and 'better communication' is a real buzz-phrase in management-speak. But how many managers, never mind employees as a whole, have been trained in communication skills? How many leaders of large organisations know how communication works? Not many, is the answer to both questions. Yet better communication in all directions, up, down and sideways, inside and outside, is absolutely the key to greater efficiency, more creativity and innovation, and happier working environments.

Why is this? To explain, I'm going to borrow an idea from General Carl von Clausewitz. In his masterpiece *On War*,[24] he describes the effect of 'friction' on the progress of war, where many difficulties accumulate to foil even the best thought-out strategy. That's how poor communication works in organisations, as an invisible friction slowing everything down, creating difficulties that needn't have existed. It consists of thousands of miscommunications including misunderstandings, misperceptions, misinformation, disinformation, failure to inform and deliberate deceptions. It's simply not possible to calculate all the damage this friction does to the smooth running of the organisational machine.

Now let's turn our attention to communication in the outside world. Everyone is becoming connected. The chat in the village street has turned into a worldwide conversation. Billions of people are now exposed to a huge variety of personalities, viewpoints and events. Individuals can interact with other people anywhere in the world, at any time. No doubt the future will bring even more options for instant access to an unlimited amount of information and contacts. Yet leaders in organisations often struggle when it comes to communication, not knowing whether to control it tightly or let it develop a life of its own.

So here's the thing. As the amount of information and knowledge in the world has grown, much of it has been hived off into specialist areas. That's perfectly logical. But it's likely that a great deal of future innovation will come from making unexpected connections between different branches of specialist knowledge. This applies as much within organisations as in society as a whole. In the future, machine algorithms will help these connections to be made.

The most likely next step for communication technology will be the development of an 'intelligent Internet'. This will give individuals the ability to tailor flows of information and communication to their own specific needs. For example, given a 'brief', algorithms will search for relevant data, filter out the junk and provide summaries and overviews. They will be responsive to the way the individual uses communication, pick up on communication elsewhere that's relevant, and make suggestions as to new channels of information.

The usefulness of this in the workplace is immediately obvious. Employees will be able to ask for help with particular areas of knowledge, skill, problem solving and so on. The intelligent Internet will supply accurate information and useful ideas from both within and outside the organisation. It will suggest people to contact or perhaps an online course that can be incorporated into the

---

24 Carl von Clausewitz, *On War* (Penguin Classics, 1984 [1832]), 164–7.

working day as a way of supplementing the employee's own knowledge. It will break down silos and eradicate 'stove-pipe' thinking.

However, all the technology in the world cannot turn people into good communicators. In an increasingly interconnected, networked world there is an urgent need for training in communication skills at all levels. Throughout the organisation, individuals need to be able to discover the strengths and weaknesses of their personal communication styles and how to express their thoughts and emotions in simple, clear language.

The convergence of more intelligent communication systems with employees skilled in techniques of interpersonal communication will create an immensely powerful field of energy. Nothing is more important to the future success of organisations than being able to improve communication in all its varied aspects. But there will be contrasting approaches to the management of communication at work.

The ENGINEERED ORGANISATION will create 'communication architectures'. The emphasis will be on ensuring that the 'right' information flows to the 'right' people. Communication will be ushered along corridors; walls and fences will be erected to block access to certain data; surveillance will ensure everyone is following the rules. With its focus on quantifiable costs and benefits, the ENGINEERED ORGANISATION will only provide training in communication to a few select employees.

The PROGRESSIVE ORGANISATION, though, will take an entirely different view. It will see that an increased flow of communication across a more interconnected workforce will improve transparency, make it easier for people to understand what's going on, and build bridges between different areas of knowledge and skill. It will encourage the growth of new networks and virtual communities; it will seek to open up access to as much information as possible to everyone; it will free up employees to communicate what they want, to whom they want, when they want, just as they do in private life. It will see open, transparent communication channels as fundamental to a culture of innovation and progress.

The role of Principled Persuaders will be to help oversee the opening up of communication channels in a way that allows a continuous feedback loop to develop. Leaders of the organisation should be in constant touch with the thoughts, ideas, emotions and experiences of employees. Using Big Data techniques, this continuous flow of information can be analysed and interpreted to provide insights on future directions, tapping into 'the wisdom of crowds'.[25]

---

25   James Surowiecki, *The Wisdom of Crowds* (Abacus, 2005).

After all, employees might turn out to be one of the very best sources of information on not only how to improve the organisation, but on markets, competitors and current and future social issues. The highly interconnected PROGRESSIVE ORGANISATION can conduct what Peter Schwartz called 'a collective enquiry into the deep structure of the business and how it is changing'.[26]

Diverging Pathways

The Five Converging Forces will reshape the world of work. But change will take place in a zigzag fashion, not in a straight line. The pace and direction of change will vary from place to place. All organisations will end up somewhere on a spectrum between the ENGINEERED and the PROGRESSIVE ORGANISATION.

In the organisation that's taken the ENGINEERED route, an elite cadre of top executives will ensure that the ever-growing mountain of data is channelled only to certain people, as well as being used to monitor every action of employees. They will replace unpredictable humans with automation and robots. Training will only be supplied to specific people for specific purposes. The latest techniques of psychological control and motivational communication will be used to produce a compliant workforce.

In the organisation that has taken the PROGRESSIVE route, leaders will be dedicated to creating a working environment in which individuals can flourish. Information will be used intelligently and openly with the focus on providing new insights and knowledge. Automation and robots will free employees up from routine work in order to provide new people-to-people services. All employees will have access to some form of continuous learning. They will be taught how to understand each other better and how to communicate face-to-face more effectively. The communication culture will be one of connecting and sharing widely across the organisation.

Which direction do you think your organisation will take?

A Clear Purpose in an Uncertain World

Only the PROGRESSIVE ORGANISATION will be in tune with the way people want to live their lives and with the way the world is changing. At work, right

---

26 Peter Schwartz, *The Art of the Long View* (Wiley, 1991), 221.

now, most people are yearning for more freedom, more stimulation, more fun, more of what makes life pleasant to live. Far too many people still go to work dreading the day ahead whether they are highly paid professionals or small cogs in a huge organisational machine. Far too many people are working well under their potential.

There is also a strategic reason for creating more PROGRESSIVE ORGANISATIONS. We're becoming what's been called a 'Heisenberg society':

> *in which the only certainty is uncertainty and constant change [where] successful development strategies will require dynamic and adaptive planning, with policies continually adjusted to a rapidly changing social and economic environment.*[27]

We're moving steadily away from an era of logic and machine-like thinking into one of complexity, uncertainty, fuzziness, where emotions will play as big a role in decision-making as rationality.

In this context, organisations that are able to create cultures of strong communication and innovation will thrive. Those that set out to impose greater controls on their workforces will not flourish. As urban studies specialist, Richard Florida, says:

> *diverse and open communities have compelling competitive advantages in stimulating creativity, generating innovations and increasing wealth and economic growth.*[28]

And there is an even more important reason why PROGRESSIVE ORGANISATIONS are the way of the future. They will have a deeper sense of purpose – a wider vision of what organisations, and the economic system they're embedded in, are for.

Around half the countries in the world have now adopted some form of capitalism.[29] There are many different varieties. It is still the case that, for many political and organisational leaders, the purpose of the economic system is to create wealth so that specific power bases can be established whether national, corporate or personal. These are the direct heirs of the

---

27 Anatole Kaletsky, *Capitalism 4.0* (Bloomsbury, 2011), 306, referring to Joshua Cooper Ramo, *The Beijing Consensus* (The Foreign Policy Centre, 2004).

28 Richard Florida, *The Rise of the Creative Class* (Basic Books, 2002), 327.

29 Mauro F. Guillén, *The Architecture of Collapse: The Global System in the 21st Century* (Clarendon Lectures in Management Studies, 2014).

nineteenth-century capitalist system with all its inequalities and injustices. If we follow these people, the twenty-first century could see us reinventing a situation where elites get the vast majority of the created wealth, squeezing out everyone else.

Thankfully, there are other leaders who believe there is little purpose in creating wealth if it enriches a few and leaves the vast majority struggling behind. Leaders are emerging who will subscribe to the view that the ultimate purpose of the economic system is:

> *to improve the health and happiness of every human being on the planet.*

This is an unashamedly humanistic view but it is an ideal that is achievable, albeit in the very long term. This is the meta-purpose behind all economic activity. More and more thought leaders are beginning to move this way. For example, Nobel Laureate economist Edmund Phelps wrote:

> *an economy enabling people's mutual pursuit of the highest good may be termed a good economy. An economy is good if and only if it permits and fosters the good life.*[30]

Exactly the same point can be made for organisations. They too have a meta-purpose, which may be expressed as follows:

> *Organisations exist in order to develop products and services that will enhance the lives of individuals and contribute towards social progress.*

This fundamental core purpose for organisations provides the basic framework around which PROGRESSIVE ORGANISATIONS can grow. But how do we get from where we are now, to a future where the majority of employees will work in PROGRESSIVE ORGANISATIONS?

That's where Principled Persuasion comes in. By changing today's Motivational Communication into Principled Persuasion, organisations will, over time, be able to transform their cultures from one of twentieth-century 'command and control' to twenty-first-century 'communicate and innovate'.

---

30 Edmund Phelps, *Mass Flourishing* (Princeton University Press, 2013), 288.

Communicate and Innovate: The Way of the Future

The implications of this type of culture change are enormous, not least for the employees themselves. As PROGRESSIVE ORGANISATIONS liberate 'power from below', employees will have to take on higher levels of personal responsibility for their thoughts and actions. In order to be truly 'autonomous', they need to become self-regulating. Principled Persuaders will help them to do this.

Communication will encourage an environment in which the employees of the future will not only take responsibility for the work they do, but also for their own destiny in terms of self-improvement, ethical behaviour, and awareness of the broader issues affecting the organisation and the world around them.

Employees at all levels will need to learn to think for themselves rather than follow others, increase their levels of attentiveness, question data and assumptions. They will learn to be cautious when easy solutions present themselves and patient enough to wait for more information. They will understand that criticism, doubt, confusion and even failure are integral parts of learning and making progress. They will gain a better understanding of how their own mind works, how to open up to and analyse other beliefs and opinions, and how to adjust their own communication styles to different circumstances.

Bear in mind that this is a vision of the future. It will take some time to get to this point. We are a long way off it at the moment. However, the Five Converging Forces will push this process along. It seems certain that future employees will be better educated, more informed, more in touch with others, more willing and more equipped to engage in stimulating, creative activity at work.

Step by Step: Into the Future

The first step towards realising this vision of future work is to agree that it is the destination to head for. Every reader of this book needs consciously to make that decision. That's because change like this can only be achieved through weight of numbers. The world is full of cynicism, inertia and vested interests. These are the enemies of progress. There has to be an intellectual and emotional commitment to the idea that the world of work is capable of being changed for the good of individuals and for society as a whole.

The second step is to begin acquiring the tools necessary to make these radical changes in organisational culture. That's why I've written this book.

There are already many thousands of professionals charged with improving communication within their organisations. They are bombarded with advice on the latest techniques for effective internal communication and how to 'engage' employees.

I say to you all, please step back for a moment, take a deep breath, and ask yourself 'what is all this communication for?' What is your ultimate objective beyond earning money and building a career, pleasing your boss?

If your answer is to help create a better society, then this is the book for you.

PART II
SIGNPOSTS FOR THE ROAD AHEAD

CHAPTER 3

Changing Minds:
The Basic Principles of
Principled Persuasion

Each attitude being a syllable in human nature's total message, it
takes the whole of us to spell the meaning out completely.[1]

The future lies with PROGRESSIVE ORGANISATIONS that have cultivated an open
communication environment where employees can share thoughts, emotions,
differences and ideas freely. For this to happen, there will need to be a radical
change of mindset on the part of senior managers and employees themselves.
This is a challenging task for Principled Persuaders.

You would have thought that it would be easy to change the minds of
intelligent, rational people when they are presented with strong arguments.
It's not. In his classic work, *The Structure of Scientific Revolutions*, Thomas
Kuhn described how hard it is to change the minds of scientists, supposedly the
most rational of people. When new ideas come along that don't fit established
paradigms, they are firmly resisted by those who have a vested interest in the
old ideas. Kuhn quotes Max Planck, the physicist who introduced quantum
theory, and said:

> *a new scientific truth does not triumph by convincing its opponents*
> *and making them see the light, but rather because its opponents*
> *eventually die, and a new generation grows up that is familiar*
> *with it.*[2]

However, Principled Persuaders are good at taking the long view. They
understand that to get from where most organisations are now, to a widespread

---

1   William James, *The Varieties of Religious Experience* (Longmans, Green & Co., 1902).
2   Thomas Kuhn, *The Structure of Scientific Revolutions* (University of Chicago Press, 1996), 151.
    Max Planck's comment is taken from his *Scientific Autobiography and Other Papers* (1949).

acceptance of the 'communicate and innovate' culture, will take some time. But you have to begin somewhere. And the place to begin is with that powerful strategic driver of change, MENTALISATION. Finding better ways of releasing what's in employees' minds is key to developing a PROGRESSIVE ORGANISATION. That's why in this chapter you're going to be taken down a trail.

The trail begins at the brain and winds its way through thoughts and emotions, nature and nurture, and the notion of self. It plunges through the thorny bushes of beliefs and attitudes and how to change behaviour. At the end of the trail we emerge into a clearing and describe the basic principles behind Principled Persuasion.

Your Interconnected Brain

There are more connections in your brain than there are particles in the universe. 100 billion neurons, the nerve cells of the brain, continuously fire off messages to each other and all parts of your body. Just one neuron can have as many as 200,000 connections. Powered by electricity, neurons release chemical neurotransmitters across a gap (the synapse) to their neighbours. That's how all communication in the brain is managed, through electrochemical activity. Right now, your brain is a seething mass of excitatory neurotransmitters, some saying go, go, go, and others, stop, stop, stop! The energy demands are so high that your brain consumes 20 per cent of your total calorie intake.

Different parts of the brain have specific functions. For example, the occipital lobe at the back of your head deals mainly in visual material, while your frontal lobe is heavily engaged in planning and making fine judgements. But the more neuroscientists explore the physical structures of the brain, the more they realise that everything is connected to everything else in ways that might never be fully understood. It's unlikely that anyone will ever fathom out how all that physical activity in the brain is converted into conscious thoughts and feelings.

What's more, the vast majority of brain activity goes on at levels well below the level of consciousness. You are constantly trying to exert executive control over your thoughts and feelings, but the vast majority of your brain's activity is well beyond your mental grasp. In responding to its environment, your brain carries out millions of electrochemical reactions before serving up a conscious thought.

Three Brains in One

The human brain has taken millions of years to evolve. Scientists describe the evolution of the brain as taking place in three phases.

First, around 200 million years ago, came the reptilian brain capable of sensing and reacting in a 'feel good', 'feel bad' way. It consists of the brainstem and cerebellum. This primitive part of your brain controls the fundamental workings of your body such as muscles that allow swallowing, your heart and lungs, and communication with your spinal cord. This is the seat of instinct and your life force. If your brainstem dies, that's it – you're gone.

Then by around 150 million years ago the limbic system that specialises in emotions and memories had formed. It contains crucial components: the thalamus that's the 'Clapham Junction' of sensory signalling to all parts of the brain; the hypothalamus that keeps your body's internal environment stable and regulates your nervous system; the hippocampus that's essential for storing and retrieving memories; the amygdala that triggers off rapid emotional responses such as fear or anger. The limbic system is in charge of much of your behaviour. Signals are relayed from the limbic system to the rest of your brain, telling you what to do.

Somewhere around 50–25 million years ago the cerebral cortex was in place. It surrounded and buried the other 'two' brains. It looks like a wrinkled walnut. Laid out flat, it would occupy the area of a tennis court. Split into two hemispheres it's responsible for all your higher order functions including thought, vision and judgement.

Of course, the evolutionary process was far more complicated than these three stages suggest. As the physical structure of the brain grew, each part was always deeply interconnected with the other. There's also the little problem that your brain is not the same as your mind. The human mind developed on a different timescale. Around one million years ago, the brain started to expand rapidly. It's estimated to have reached its current structure about 200,000 years ago, having doubled in size over a two-million-year period. That's the period during which the human mind would have expanded its capabilities well beyond the other animals', culminating in language about 150,000 years ago.

Yet the story of the triune brain serves a purpose. It tells you that all your thoughts and feelings are governed by a complex interplay of reasoning, emotions and instinctive reactions.

Reasonable Emotions

For a very long time, at least since the Enlightenment in the eighteenth century, reason was seen as a higher power that differentiated us from the animals. Despite Darwin's discovery of our animal origins, reason has continued to be set on a pedestal whereas emotions are seen as unhelpful to decision-making.

Freud's investigations into the subconscious seemed to provide further evidence that deep emotional impulses controlled behaviour. It was as if emotions were like hot, bubbling lava deep in the volcano of our minds, liable to burst out at any time, burying rational thought. But, according to modern science, another metaphor might be more accurate. In this scenario, emotions are like deep subterranean rivers continuously rising to the surface, mingling invisibly with the flow of rational thought.

In the 1990s, Daniel Goleman brought the idea of 'emotional intelligence' to people's attention.[3] He set out to show how emotions play an important role in thought and decision-making. He said that people with characteristics such as self-awareness, control over impulses, empathy and social skills were more likely to be successful.

Since then, neuroscientists have made further progress in identifying the way the emotional system in the brain is interconnected with the areas involved in rational decision-making. One leading scientist has concluded: 'higher cortical functions, particularly those located in the evolutionarily advanced prefrontal cortex, are critical to emotion.'[4] There seems to be plenty of evidence to prove this point.

Here are some examples. Neurons have thin, spindly fibres called axons that reach out to other nerve cells; the more axons you have connecting the left prefrontal lobe to the amygdala, the more resilient you are likely to be. Low electrochemical activity in the hippocampus means you are less likely to be sensitive to the social context in which you find yourself. High levels of activity in the insula, a region of the brain deep in the cerebral cortex, means you have a high level of self-awareness. If you have a positive outlook on life, it's likely that your prefrontal cortex and nucleus accumbens are whirring away. Differences in brain structure and activity explain why individuals react completely differently to the same stimuli, including messages.

But what is common to everyone is that the rational and emotional parts of the brain are inextricably interlinked. They always work together.

---

3   Daniel Goleman, *Emotional Intelligence* (Bloomsbury, 1996).
4   Richard Davidson with Sharon Begley, *The Emotional Life of Your Brain* (Hodder, 2012), xv.

This presents a real challenge to those who think you need to keep emotions out of decision-making and organisational life in general. You can't. You can pretend you are keeping emotions at bay, and you can certainly hide them, but they are always there, working away to influence how you think. Naturally, we all need to learn how to hold back strong emotions at certain times. We're taught this as children, or should be. But it can be difficult. The eyes are the windows of the brain. In certain situations, they send signals straight to the more primitive emotional networks provoking thoughtless reactions.

Yet feelings permeate everything you do. They are useful guides to the way you think and behave. Difficult decisions, where pros and cons balance out, are often resolved by some kind of 'gut feel'. Emotions build on rational assessment to give you a feeling of rightness – 'Yes, that's it – that's what I'll do'. They evolved to protect us from harm.

The lesson here for persuaders is that even a highly rational presentation of arguments touches on people's emotions. When Principled Persuaders set out to tap into people's emotions, they do not see this as an underhand way of manipulating their minds. On the contrary, they see emotions as a valuable aid to judgement. Until recently, it would have been unthinkable for organisations to measure their employees' emotions. But in the progressive organisation new ways of measuring and managing emotions will become an intrinsic part of the communication culture.

Nature or Nurture?

It's an old controversy. Were you born the way you are, or made that way? It's obvious you must be a product of your genes, but to what extent are your inherited characteristics modified by your environment? Extreme views have been put forward on this subject. Francis Galton, who early in the twentieth century sparked off a sinister craze for eugenics,[5] believed that all aspects of the human psyche were inherited. By contrast, behaviourists, like John Watson,[6] believed that, given the right environment, any human being could be moulded to become any type of person. It's worth quoting what he said:

---

5   Eugenics (good breeding) was based on the belief that as people inherited their characters, only the 'best' people should be allowed to breed. This idea caught on in many countries, including the United States where 30 states introduced sterilisation programmes. When the Nazis copied American ideas, eugenics fell quickly out of favour.

6   John Broadus Watson (1878–1958) was the father of the American school of psychology known as behaviourism.

Give me a dozen healthy infants ... and my own specified world to bring them up in and I'll guarantee to take any one at random and train him to become any type of specialist I might select – doctor, lawyer, artist, merchant-chief and, yes, even beggar-man and thief, regardless of his talents, penchants, tendencies, abilities, vocations, and race of his ancestors.

The truth appears to be somewhere between these two extremes. Scientists now see evolution working as a continuous feedback loop between genes and the environment. It's estimated that between 30 and 50 per cent of personal characteristics are inherited, and that environment accounts for between 50 70 per cent of the difference between individuals. Some evidence for this was provided by the curious case of neuroscientist, Professor James Fallon. He announced to the world in 2013 that he had discovered his brain had all the neurological hallmarks of a psychopathic killer. Yet this 66-year-old family man had never been involved in any violent incident. As he pointed out, genes need to be switched on by experiences.

Your personal development, then, is in many ways an arbitrary process. It's a result of particular genes interacting with particular environments, producing a characteristic set of beliefs and attitudes that help you to survive and prosper in the best way you can. It's a classic chicken and egg situation: as one philosopher put it: 'The world appears the way it does because we are the way we are, and we are the way we are because we have evolved in a world the way it is'.[7]

Who Are You?

So far we've established that you're a unique product of your brain's structure and networks, your genes, the environment in which you were brought up and the conditions in which you live now. The continuous flow of sensations into your brain since you were a foetus has given you your individuality. Not one person in the world at any point in history will have been exactly like you.

But this raises another question. Who are you really? The problem is, you have many selves. To start with, you have an inner and an outer self. Your inner self is composed of all your thoughts and emotions that you never give voice

---

7   R.N. Shephard quoted in Henry Plotkin, *Necessary Knowledge* (Oxford University Press, 2007), 138.

to. Your outer self is a very social one, which you train to play different parts in different contexts.

Your inner self is very precious. Consisting of your deepest beliefs, attitudes, values, emotions, perceptions, needs and hopes, this self needs protection. You can become very upset if anyone suggests that any of these deep drivers are misguided or plain wrong. Yet, for your outer, social self, you edit these inner features and show the world what you think it is appropriate to show at any one time. This editing process is based on your judgement of what you think is needed in that particular situation. People in organisations often hide their true beliefs.

Then there's your changing self. It would be strange if you showed exactly the same characteristics at 60 as at 16. Experience has a major impact on the kind of person you become. As you grow older, you change your identity by affiliating yourself with ways of thinking and behaving that seem appropriate at the time. Your responses to family, friends, peer group and different role models continually adjust, often without you being aware of what's happening.

There's yet another self – the one you have very little control over. This self is the product of other people's opinions about you. Their judgements are made on the basis of what you look like, what you do, what beliefs and attitudes you decide to reveal. Whether you seem to like the things they do. Their perceptions of you may be correct or utterly false. Many people you deal with every day will have a distorted view of who you really are. No wonder it's so hard to predict people's behaviour, even when you think you know them well.

So that's how it is. In many ways the world we live in is one of a succession of mirages and illusions. What it comes down to is that you are a bundle of different selves. Looking for your essential 'I' is, as Julian Baggini[8] memorably put it, 'like trying to eat your own face'.

None of this matters if things are going along just fine. For the PROGRESSIVE ORGANISATION what matters most is that an environment is created in which people can be open about their beliefs, and willing to exchange different perspectives with others. You should be able to reveal more of your inner selves.

Believe What You Like

Imagine for a moment you were born in Africa in 10,000 BC, or in China during the Ming Dynasty, or Great Britain in the sixteenth century. Would you hold

---

8   Julian Baggini, *The Ego Trick* (Granta Books, 2011), 121.

the same deep beliefs as you hold now? Of course not. The idea is laughable. Yet everyone holds their deepest beliefs to be true, although it's evident that others hold opposite beliefs that they also hold to be true. So why is this important for organisations? At a fundamental level, cultural progress comes from different belief systems rubbing up against each other. Often it leads to conflict, but far more often, different belief systems meld into each other, creating something new. That's why diversity, not conformity, is so crucial to organisational success.

As you grow, your genetic inheritance is modified by your experiences and sensations. Parents, teachers, friends, peers, mentors and role models all influence your beliefs. You wrap them around you like a blanket to protect you from a cold and heartless world. Those beliefs are your personal and unique interpretation of the way the world is. This is, what psychologists call, your 'schema'. These foundational beliefs are the basis for most of your behaviour. They are well adjusted to your need to survive and prosper, otherwise you wouldn't hold them.

Many of the beliefs you hold are unproven or false. After all, you can't check out everything you believe to be true. Nor do you think hard about every belief you hold. There's just not enough time. Anyway, even if some of your beliefs are false, it doesn't really matter if things are going along well for you. Our day-to-day lives don't require us to be certain about everything we believe. But it does matter in organisations. False beliefs, whether about the organisation, other people, or perhaps even your own capabilities are, like poor communication, another major hidden obstacle to progress.

False beliefs in organisations need correcting to enable people to work more effectively together. The only way to achieve this is by stimulating a continuous conversation that exposes people to everyone else's perspectives. This is a key strategic objective for Principled Persuaders – to foster continuous discussion in an atmosphere of openness and transparency. As different beliefs are shared, new ideas can emerge from the interplay of different perspectives.

Changing False Beliefs

Within a culture of open discussion, there are three main ways of changing people's false beliefs.

The first is to make new information widely available. For example, many employees may have a range of negative perceptions about senior managers. If they are false beliefs, they can be countered by providing more information on the personalities involved, their skills and achievements, their rewards and so on. New information is a powerful tool: if it gets people thinking about an issue that can be enough by itself to change perspectives.

The second method involves 'conflict resolution'. This means encouraging opposing beliefs to come up against each other. This can only happen in an environment where people are allowed to be honest, and where views can be aired without any kind of threat. As we all know, this is not the case in many organisations. People often keep their views to themselves for fear of exposing themselves to ridicule or negative, even aggressive, reactions.

The third method is the use of persuasive language that taps into people's imaginations and emotions. You can alter perspectives by changing the vocabulary used to describe a particular issue. One of the key tasks of Principled Persuaders is to broaden the organisation's vocabulary. They will take a thorny issue and re-describe it. They will use metaphors to build a bridge between one situation and another so people can quickly understand, intellectually and emotionally, what's being said. I'll explore this aspect of persuasion in more detail in Chapter 8.

Watch Your Attitude

Attitudes are the way you show your beliefs to the world. They are your public stance. In fact, that's what the word 'attitude' originally meant. In Dr Johnson's dictionary of 1755 attitude is 'the posture or action in which a statue or painted figure is placed'. By the nineteenth century, the word 'attitude' was being used in the sense of 'settled behaviour, or manner of acting, as representative of opinion or feeling'.

In 1935, the psychologist G.W. Allport declared attitude to be social psychology's most distinctive and indispensable concept. He defined it as:

> a mental and neural state of readiness, organised through experience, exerting a directive or dynamic influence upon the individual's response to all objects and situations with which it is related.

That means your beliefs predispose you to take up certain mental positions as you encounter different experiences.

When you think of attitudes as the mental positions you take on everything you encounter in life, it's immediately obvious you must have many thousands of them. And, as soon as you start to voice them in the shape of opinions, they tell other people what kind of person you are. That's what they're for. They are your personal public address system.

Another way of looking at attitudes is to see them as practical tools. You could see them as knives that help you cut your way though the jungle of everyday existence. I'm for this and against that. For someone who is completely and always honest, attitudes are a direct reflection of deeper beliefs. But for the rest of us, they are a more flexible tool than that. They allow you to dress yourself up verbally for different occasions. The attitudes you express to friends about work can be very different from those you express to your colleagues. Your different selves are perfectly capable of voicing different attitudes to suit different occasions. After all, organisations are full of people paying 'lip service' to statements with which they do not agree, just to get along.

Some attitudes, though, are not to be trifled with. These are the attitudes that reflect our deepest beliefs about who we are. They are likely to be well thought through, linked to strong emotions and based on personal experience. Extreme attitudes are also hard to budge. On the other hand, it's relatively easy to change people's weakly held attitudes, especially if they don't care much one way or the other about a particular issue.

If you're a self-monitoring type of person, which all Principled Persuaders should be, keep a watch on your own attitudes as you go through the day. Identify the ones that are important to you and those that don't matter so much. This will help you to realise why communication designed to change attitudes is so often ineffective. It's only when the communication is right on target, addresses an attitude that's important to you, and provides you with convincing new information, that it stands any chance of changing it. That's why the vast majority of public communication has the effect of reinforcing attitudes rather than changing them.

Measuring Attitudes in Organisations

Measuring attitudes can be a poor guide to deeper beliefs, and an even worse guide to behaviour. A classic study carried out in the United States in 1934 illustrates this point. Richard LaPiere, professor of sociology at Stanford University, sent a young Chinese couple out to dine at 66 hotels and 184 restaurants. Just one of these establishments refused to serve them. Afterwards, LaPiere wrote to all the patrons of the places visited and asked 'Will you accept members of the Chinese race as guests?' Ninety-two per cent of those who replied said they would not. It may not have been the soundest piece of research, but it highlighted the incontrovertible fact that people often say one thing and do another.

There is no absolutely foolproof way of being able to predict people's actions on the basis of their attitudes. Researchers Ajzen and Fishbein[9] pointed out that the more specific the attitude, the greater the possibility of prediction. For example, 'I think coffee is a delicious drink' would seem to predict coffee drinking. Yet there's the possibility that another belief will intervene to stop the action, for example, 'caffeine is bad for my headaches'.

So if attitudes are so unreliable as a guide to beliefs and actions, why do organisations spend so much time and money measuring them? The answer is that, for a time, they have provided the best information that can be gathered on what employees think and feel about their working environments. The annual attitude survey has done a sterling job since it became commonplace in the 1990s. It has helped organisations get a fix on areas of strength and weakness and, if properly followed through, led to real improvements. But it's time to move on.

In the PROGRESSIVE ORGANISATION, Principled Persuaders will provide the fuel for open discussion of the major issues by tapping into continuous feedback from employees, using the latest communication technologies. Rather than asking employees to tick boxes with agreement or disagreement to statements, you could start to think about how to use Big Data analytics to make sense of an unceasing stream of information.

There are already numerous devices through which employees can send their opinions and feelings at any time of day or night. Digital social networks have sprung up in many organisations. Simple software is available for employees to conduct their own surveys. The technologies are already here and more will be appearing. What's missing is support from senior managers to go down this route.

Yet this will change as more and more of them realise that looking at data that come from annual attitude surveys is like studying a fossil. It will become obvious that this kind of data is too slow and too late to be of any real strategic value. Organisations need to begin tapping into digital-savvy research companies that are experts in the use of text analysis, algorithms, graphic presentation and other techniques that will turn the 'wisdom of the crowd' into hard information that can be acted upon.

Principled Persuaders will need to be in the forefront of these new ways of accessing information from employees: not just attitudes, but deeper beliefs, emotions, ideas, predictions and general observations. Their aim will be to

---

9   Icek Ajzen and Martin Fishbein, *Understanding Attitudes and Predicting Social Behaviour* (Prentice Hall, 1980), 30–31.

create a constant feedback loop in real time, all the time – now that really would be a 'learning organisation'.[10]

It's What People *Do* That Matters

Measuring attitudes, beliefs and emotions in organisations in the way described above will enable the PROGRESSIVE ORGANISATION to keep a finger on the pulse of cultural life. That's not enough in itself to guarantee a strong movement towards a happier, more innovative working environment. It will be necessary to change the way senior managers and employees behave. Here are five ways of changing behaviour. Only the last two of them are of direct interest to Principled Persuaders.

The first is force. Of course, the PROGRESSIVE ORGANISATION will reject this method, but it's worth dwelling on just for a moment. At one extreme, say in totalitarian societies, violent coercion supported by propaganda, creates a climate within which many people have to bury their true beliefs. They voice attitudes that will get them through and demonstrate they are no threat to the regime by behaving as they're expected to. Of course, to various degrees, there are organisations like this too, where a culture of fear prevails.

The next main method of stimulating change is through incentives, material and emotional. The reward system is the root of all organisational behaviour: not just salaries, but bonuses, incentive schemes, company welfare, career promotions, even training and development contribute to the reward culture. To change behaviour in an organisation, it is often enough to attach some form of reward, such as money or recognition.

A practical way of changing behaviour is to change the conditions in which people work. There are numerous theories about this, and there have been many attempts to create more people-friendly workplaces. But the fact remains that in most offices and factories the demands of efficiency triumph over those of humanity. How employees behave during the working day is conditioned by such factors as whether they can personalise the space around them, how much they can move around, ambient noise, lighting and ventilation, even the shape of their desk and chair.

The fourth route to behaviour change, which is firmly in the domain of Principled Persuasion, is to adopt techniques of clinical psychology such as 'Cognitive Behavioural Therapy' (CBT). Clinicians start by identifying an individual's prevailing beliefs and attitudes, the 'schema'. They investigate this

---

10   A term made famous by Peter Senge in *The Fifth Discipline* (Random House, 1990).

cluster of interconnected core beliefs about the self, the nature of the world, significant relationships and what might happen in the future. The process of 'cognitive restructuring' then begins. Patients are asked to detail the situations and thoughts causing them problems. They will be urged to produce some evidence to support their negative thoughts. Gentle probing and questioning gets them to start challenging their own thinking. In this way they can be led to change their damaging habits of thought and begin to take positive actions to improve their lives. I'm not suggesting that Principled Persuaders become clinical psychologists, but undoubtedly there is huge scope for improvements in interpersonal communication within organisations.

The fifth method of changing behaviour is through the presentation of arguments and open debate. It is a great mistake to think that simply coming up with a strong and sensible reason for something, and then presenting the argument, will be enough to change behaviour. It won't. This is communicating on, what some academics call, 'the transmission model'[11] – the dominant model behind Motivational Communication. It comes from a way of thinking that says: 'let's put some communication out there that increases trust in management and makes people feel good about the work they're doing'.

By contrast, Principled Persuasion is based on an interactive model of communication, akin to CBT. Its higher goal is not to motivate, nor even to 'engage', but to create a true communication partnership with all employees. It works by crafting a communication environment within which employees can think through the issues and persuade themselves of what needs to be done. It involves training people to present their arguments clearly, ask the right questions, and listen hard.

So the Principled Persuader acts as a catalyst of open debate. With senior management in support, people are enabled to air their thoughts and emotions without fear of penalty. They open up to each other as mutually respectful colleagues. Diversity of thinking is encouraged, not conformity to the prevailing organisational culture. Established patterns of thought are challenged and argued out. This is how progress is achieved. This is the way that Principled Persuaders can change organisational behaviour for the better.

The Basic Principles of Principled Persuasion

Let's pause for a moment and reflect.

---

11 See Jesse Sostrin, *Remaking Communication at Work* (Palgrave Macmillan, 2013).

Our senses are the gateway to our consciousness, our entire being. Mediated by our incredibly complex brains, the raw material of sensory experience is converted into our deepest beliefs. Not everyone interprets the same sensory experiences in the same way. Each person has a unique way of looking at the world. Thank goodness. Otherwise we would all be 'sense-machines', agreeing on everything. Despite predictable reflexes and other common psychological features, the essence of humanity, as opposed to the rest of the animal kingdom, is that we can all go off in a multitude of different directions. What makes us human are our differences, not our similarities – they are what we have inherited from our animal ancestors. So what Principled Persuaders should be doing is not to get everyone to think the same way, but to encourage difference, diversity and debate.

Underlying all the principles below is the idea that Principled Persuaders stimulate cultural change by enabling an organisation-wide conversation. They change minds by creating an environment in which employees are empowered to change their own minds, to persuade themselves that there's a better way of doing things.

The principles below deliberately ignore Machiavellian persuasive techniques. They also ignore techniques designed to gain a quick advantage or make a superficial impression. They are not about selling. They are the foundations upon which Principled Persuaders can build a PROGRESSIVE ORGANISATION. They are the first of seven sets of principles described in this book, all of which, working together, will help you devise a plan for progressive culture change in your organisation.

Principle 1: Know what it is you're aiming for
What do you want to happen as a result of your persuasion? You need to have a clear picture of what needs to be done to turn your organisation into a PROGRESSIVE one. Use the descriptions of the PROGRESSIVE ORGANISATION given in Chapter 2 to help you.

Principle 2: Tune into what's on people's minds
Don't rely on conventional attitude surveys. Set up a new way of receiving and analysing constant 24/7 feedback from employees on their beliefs, attitudes, emotions and ideas. This will require management support and investment.

Principle 3: Present issues for discussion
Using the continuous employee feedback, highlight the subjects that people most want to talk about and begin putting together

communication material and forums (digital and real) that allow people to exchange different perspectives on the most important issues.

Principle 4: Feed back in the areas of agreement and disagreement and provide guidance

Do this by producing informative material that covers the main arguments. Provide guidance on the pros and cons of particular courses of action so people can think things through for themselves. Describe emotional as well as rational benefits. If possible, use trusted and authoritative sources to provide evidence that the desired courses of action will work. Show how they benefit individual employees as well as the organisation as a whole.

OK. So what's next? It's time to turn to a hot topic – why and how to cultivate a working environment where employees can be happy – yes, that's the word – happy.

CHAPTER 4

Happiness at Work: The Principles of Hedonic Persuasion

No one can be perfectly happy till all are happy.[1]

Is it too ridiculous to imagine that, one day, the world will be full of PROGRESSIVE ORGANISATIONS whose employees enjoy their working lives just as much as their leisure time? And, what's more, that their happiness at work has the direct result of making their organisations more successful? Principled Persuaders don't think these ideas are ridiculous. They know that a key objective of Principled Persuasion is to raise levels of happiness throughout the workforce.

Employees' happiness at work is good for business. In recent years there has been an outpouring of books and articles on the subject of happiness. That's because there's a need to move beyond the concepts of 'job satisfaction' and 'well-being'. Job satisfaction, which we'll explore in more detail later, is a limited measure that revolves around the work itself. 'Well-being' is a rather artificial concept favoured by psychologists. When you're on your deathbed, your nearest and dearest won't ask you whether you had a life full of well-being; they'll hope you'll say you've led a happy life.

'Happiness' is back in fashion as a word that summarises what employees should be feeling as they go about their daily tasks at work. As you would expect there's been plenty of research on this subject. Even the most commercially minded, profit-oriented managers might be impressed by the literature on the relationship between happy employees and successful organisations. Some of this research[2] describes how the happiest workers spend 78 per cent of their time focused on their work compared with the unhappiest at only 53 per cent.

---

1   Herbert Spencer, *Social Statics* (The Online Library of Liberty, [1851]), 276.
2   Jessica Pryce-Jones, *Happiness at Work* (Wiley-Blackwell, 2010), 25.

It's also claimed that the happiest employees are 47 per cent more productive than the least happy. Other research in laboratories has shown that positive, happy people are better than unhappy people at processing information and being able to adapt to wider perspectives. Whereas a happy marriage gives the biggest boost to happiness, job dissatisfaction is a prime cause of unhappiness.[3]

Happiness is good for your health too.[4] People with high levels of 'psychological well-being' have lower levels of cortisol, a hormone associated with poor cognitive functioning, decreased muscle tissue and too much fat. Happier people have lower levels of Interleukin 6, a messenger protein, too much of which can cause heart disease and some types of cancer.

OK, so it makes good commercial and organisational sense to have happy employees, but what do you mean by 'happy'? (I hear you ask.) Well, the word happy is an interesting one. Most people would associate it with a state of joy or pleasurable activity. In fact 'happy' is more about good fortune than pleasurable sensation. The word 'happiness' derives from old English: 'happ' meant chance, fortune, what happens. Happiness happens as a result of good things happening to you. You're not in total control of this. The deliberate pursuit of happiness can lead down blind alleys. But happiness is not mysterious: you know when you're happy and when you're not.

In order for people to be happy at work, the conditions need to be right. Leaders in PROGRESSIVE ORGANISATIONS understand that these conditions have to be created – they won't spring up by themselves. That's where Principled Persuaders come in. Working with colleagues they purposefully set out to change the prevailing culture. They aim to strengthen all the aspects of work that increase happiness, and weaken or eradicate those that cause people harm. They are helped in that task by the fact that, for decades, psychologists have been exploring the factors that make people happy and unhappy at work. These are now well known and the next two chapters draw on this knowledge.

Six Sources of Happiness

Imagine for a moment a long, wide and deep flowing river. As it wends its way through the countryside it's fed by six large tributaries, each of which, in turn,

---

3   M.H. Benin and B.C. Nierstedt, 'Happiness in Single and Dual Earner Families: The Effects of Marital Happiness, Job Satisfaction and Life Cycle', *Journal of Marriage and the Family* (1985), 47.

4   See Ivan Robertson and Cary Cooper, *Well-Being: Productivity and Happiness at Work* (Palgrave Macmillan, 2011).

is supplied by a variety of smaller streams. The tributaries and smaller streams are interlinked, forming a complex system that feeds the main river. This is the 'river of happiness'. Every day the river rises and falls. In the course of your life, sensations of happiness will ebb and flow. On especially wonderful occasions your happiness may overflow. At other times you may feel sad or melancholy without even knowing why. When that next happens, use what follows to identify which sources of happiness have dried up. Each of the six large tributaries has a name:

- love;
- self-esteem;
- control;
- pleasure;
- progress;
- comfort.

These are the six sources of happiness. When they are all flowing strongly you are likely to be very happy indeed. Let's take a closer look at them.

Love

When asked what were the criteria for a healthy personality, Sigmund Freud's terse answer was '*Lieben und arbeiten*' – love and work. Love is perhaps not a word you would normally associate with the workplace, although surveys[5] have shown that 62 per cent of women and 71 per cent of men have had an affair with a colleague! Nevertheless, 'love' in its broadest sense of caring, compassion, kindness, warmth, understanding, friendliness and so on is essential to the nurturing of productive, happy working relationships.

Everyone likes belonging to a community where they feel accepted and liked. People chat, gossip and share experiences. They build friendships, some of which go beyond working hours. In fact, 42 per cent of respondents in a survey agreed that 'my most important relationships are at work'.[6] It's pleasing to find people that share your views and attitudes to life. All this gives a sense of place and purpose.

The PROGRESSIVE ORGANISATION's culture of friendliness, warmth and understanding fosters contact between people from different parts of the

---

5   Nick Isles, *Joy of Work*, report by the Work Foundation (2004), 6.
6   Isles, *Joy of Work*, 16.

organisation. This, in turn, has a direct impact on innovation and creativity. Recent research[7] has confirmed that creative, innovative ideas are often the result of meeting people outside your usual group. They may have different ways of doing things which they take for granted but are new to you and your group. Or they may have different beliefs and behaviours that you don't want to copy but stimulate you to think freshly about a particular subject. At the heart of creativity and innovation is finding new combinations of thoughts and practices. This can only happen in an organisation where people are encouraged to mix and mingle.

The idea that social relationships are important to creativity is not new. Back in 1848 John Stuart Mill said:

> It is hardly possible to overrate the value ... of placing human beings in contact with persons dissimilar to themselves and with modes of thought and action unlike those with which they are familiar.[8]

In modern jargon this is called 'living at the intersection of different social worlds'. ENGINEERED ORGANISATIONS are full of 'silos', different compartments sealed off, often by antagonism, from other groups. PROGRESSIVE ORGANISATIONS, by contrast, cultivate warm, sharing relationships.

Experiencing the different dimensions of love at work encourages people to be more co-operative, to work more productively with each other. If people like each other, and reciprocate on a tit-for-tat basis, friendly co-operation will be achieved. Co-operation fosters better understanding of each other's needs. Lack of co-operation often stems from people not liking or understanding each other – they just can't see the mutual benefits of co-operating. The funny thing is that the desire to co-operate is deep within our natures. That's how humans evolved and learned to survive. So in organisations where co-operation between employees is poor, they must have really worked hard to build barriers between a naturally co-operative species.

To many managers the idea of 'caring' for members of your team can sound a bit soft, just another of those 'feel good' but slightly woolly corporate values. Yet caring is vital for good interpersonal communication between colleagues and managers. It's impossible to train people to care. You need to foster a culture in which caring comes naturally and isn't seen as a waste of valuable time. This is particularly important at line manager level. In many

---

7   Ronald S. Burt, 'Structural Holes and Good Ideas', *AJS* 110(2) (2004), 349–99.
8   J.S. Mill, *Principles of Political Economy* (Online Library of Economics and Liberty, [1848]), Book 3, Chapter 17, 14.

organisations the reason it's so hard to get line managers to communicate well is the lack of emphasis on the personal, caring dimension. Instead the language is all about 'feedback' and 'assessment'. One of the biggest step-changes to be accomplished in the PROGRESSIVE ORGANISATION is a change of mindset by managers at all levels – they should really care about their team members' states of mind and body.

Self-Esteem

Self-esteem is the value you place upon yourself. If you have high levels of self-esteem you are more likely to look positively on life and find it meaningful. You'll be more resilient, able to bounce back from the jolts, strains and knock-backs of daily life. You're less likely to be affected by negative moods and upset by negative comments. In other words, people with good levels of self-esteem are much more likely to be better operators.

So what helps to build self-esteem at work? Obviously, recognition and praise is crucial. From the often repeated 'well done' to the more formal systems of recognition and reward, the PROGRESSIVE ORGANISATION goes out of its way to ensure that every employee feels their work is appreciated. Principled Persuasion supports this by communicating continuously the achievements of individuals and teams. This would seem obvious but it can't be taken for granted. Survey after survey reveals far too many people in organisations feel their work and personal contribution goes unrecognised.

Fair treatment is also crucial to self-esteem. Fairness is about balance. You have your own subjective sense of what is fair or unfair. To make that judgement you weigh up many different factors. In organisations there are three main areas where fairness comes to the fore: the application of rules, the way people are treated by those higher up the hierarchy, and allocation of resources. Fair rules need to be fairly applied. It's frustrating when someone playing by the rules sees someone else gain advantage by breaking them. Treating people with respect, even if they are much lower in the hierarchy than you, is fundamental to a caring organisation. As far as the allocation of resources are concerned, people look to see whether someone else with comparable levels of effort, skills and achievement is getting more help. At root, the perception of unfairness derives from a sense of loss – that we're missing out on something that should be ours.

Another major factor in an individual employee's self-esteem is the degree to which the job is seen as worthwhile and the organisation is perceived to have a good reputation. Both of these qualities relate to core purpose. In 1997, a survey[9] into whether employees saw their work as a 'job', 'career' or 'calling' found the sample split roughly into three equal thirds. The third of employees describing work as a 'calling' had the highest levels of life and job satisfaction. This is not surprising. You probably know the story. There are three men working on a construction site of a new church. An interested passer-by goes up to them and asks 'what are you doing?' The first replies 'I'm laying bricks'; the second 'I'm building a wall'; the third 'I'm praising God'. It's all about perspective.

As was pointed out in Chapter 2, organisations exist in order to develop products and services that enhance the lives of individuals and contribute towards social progress. Principled Persuasion is there to spell out the higher purposes of your organisation's work. It should show how it contributes to society as a whole and give clear examples of how it is meeting its social responsibilities. This will help to give people the feeling that they are part of something much bigger than themselves – something that is helping to move society on.

Control

This touches on one of the central themes of this book – the extent to which you, as an individual employee, are in control of your work, as opposed to being controlled by others. Our need to feel in control is a direct result of the dangerous environment in which we evolved. Brains evolved to help us maintain some degree of control over the physical world. Tools accelerated this process. As the forebrain developed, it allowed us to plan ahead, think of options, change direction if things went wrong. Control of self and others reduced risk and increased certainty. Numerous psychological studies have found that when you feel you are in control there is a positive effect on health and happiness. You feel more motivated, able to get on with life, get things done. On the other hand, having few opportunities for control generates anxiety and uncertainty.

In the PROGRESSIVE ORGANISATION, control is devolved down. That's what 'empowerment' should mean, giving people control. As described in Chapter 2, the strategic drivers of change – INFORMATION, AUTOMATION

---

9   Amy Wrzesniewski, Clark McCauley, Paul Rozin and Barry Schwartz, 'Jobs, Careers and Callings: People's Reactions to Their Work', *Journal of Research in Personality* 31 (1997), 21–33.

and EDUCATION – will provide many more new opportunities for employees to gain control over their field of operations. More control means a greater sense of achievement – a greater sense of achievement means higher levels of satisfaction and happiness. The feeling that you are achieving things correlates with progressive concepts such as autonomy, individualism, self-expression and self-determination.

Control over work, and a strong sense of achievement, are both features of craftsmanship. Thanks to new technologies, craftsmanship is making a comeback. The essence of craftsmanship lies in the desire to do something well for its own sake using tools skilfully and aiming for the highest quality. Once only manual workers used tools for the bulk of their work. Now everyone, including senior managers, needs to acquire a range of new skills in the use of technological tools. Craft-satisfaction can potentially be enjoyed by a large proportion of the workforce, especially in the PROGRESSIVE ORGANISATION where EDUCATION is a permanent feature of life at work.

Research shows people derive happiness from using existing skills and learning new ones. It can be as satisfying to use personal skills at work as during leisure time. When you're playing any kind of game, for example, the enjoyment comes from the challenge. Not too much, not too little: the game needs to be stretching but achievable. Your desire to exercise control and mastery over what you're doing goes very deep.

Another aspect of control comes from what psychologists call 'environmental clarity'. That means understanding what is going on around you both in terms of your job and the wider organisation. Good communication is essential to environmental clarity. At the interpersonal level, managers and individuals on their teams should be in continuous dialogue to reduce confusions, uncertainties and ambiguities. At the broader organisational level, there needs to be constant communication on successes, difficulties and future plans.

Surveys reveal that the level of trust in management can be very low, often less than half of all employees. Poor communication is the primary reason for this. Many organisations are far too tight in the information they release. No one expects confidential or commercially sensitive information to be distributed to all and sundry. But if employees are not being kept informed of who's who, who does what, future plans, difficulties ahead and so on, levels of trust are bound to be low. The rule of thumb should be to communicate truthfully and honestly – spell out the issues so people understand and feel more in control of their own futures. That's what Principled Persuaders will do.

Pleasure

What's the best thing to do if you're feeling a bit depressed? Go out of your way to have a pleasurable experience. It hardly matters what: a brisk walk, a cup of tea, maybe an ice-cream or watch some comedy clips on YouTube. It may not always work, but the fastest way to cheer yourself up is by having some fun. That's what clinical psychologists prescribe for people with serious bouts of depression. Experiencing pleasant events is a fundamental source of happiness. So how do you make that happen at work?

Variety, as they say, is the spice of life. Measuring the amount of variety in a job is a good way of predicting the level of satisfaction it gives. People love variety and it's good for your brain – it keeps it lively and responsive. The great economist Adam Smith recognised this back in 1766. He wrote: 'When the mind is employed about a variety of objects it is somehow expanded and enlarged'.[10] Modern psychologists agree. They've found that lack of variety at work is unpleasant and associated with negative moods, even depression. People with routine jobs have their own ways of dealing with this. They introduce their own variety, maybe by setting themselves little targets to introduce an element of game playing; or they might sing to themselves, chat to others, go for a walkabout if they can. Well designed jobs, with plenty of variety, avoid all these distractions and allow people to get more enjoyment from their work.

People derive a great deal of pleasure from being involved in creative activities. Creativity at work can take many forms including finding new ways of applying skills, acquiring new skills, solving problems and thinking about how to improve jobs and processes. Techniques such as brainstorming and lateral thinking can be enlisted to challenge established orthodoxies, the accepted way of doing things. Having a chance to be creative is fun and pleasurable for many people. In the PROGRESSIVE ORGANISATION, with its 'communicate and innovate' culture, creativity becomes a way of life.

There is another aspect of gaining pleasure from work which has come to the fore in recent years. This is the concept of 'flow'. In 1997 Mihály Csikszentmihalyi explained how people who are well motivated and competent can get into 'flow' when engaged in a task. This involves being in a state of deep concentration. You become so absorbed in a task that you forget about time and are oblivious to what's happening in the immediate environment. Coming out of flow feels like waking up, re-emerging into the 'real world'. Flow

---

10 From lectures by Adam Smith delivered at the University of Glasgow and reported by a student in 1763, quoted in John Cunningham Wood (ed.), *Adam Smith Critical Assessments* (Routledge, 1996), 166.

is probably one of the highest forms of pleasurable activity, a major contributor to happiness. Losing yourself in a task is a great way to find satisfaction. You feel you're fulfilling your potential and confirming your own sense of worth.

Progress

One of the largest sources of happiness is the feeling that you are making progress in life.[11] The ability to imagine the future distinguishes humans from all other animals. Our brains evolved with the ability not just to plan ahead, but to fantasise. We all have dreams of what life might be like if all goes well. Dreams and fantasies are pleasurable in themselves. Psychologists estimate that you spend up to 15 per cent of your entire day thinking about the future, from worrying about such things as what you're going to have for dinner to what the next step in your career might be.

You derive enormous satisfaction from setting yourself goals. This strengthens your sense of purpose. They need to be your goals, not those set for you by others. And nowhere is this more important than in the realm of self-development. Personal development is central to happiness at work. Survey after survey confirms this. In a 2004 survey[12] it was found that employees' perceptions of their organisation's emphasis on staff development correlated highly with average overall job satisfaction.[13] That means the more the organisation provides learning opportunities, the happier the workforce. Lots of learning, lots of training, lots of opportunities to acquire new skills are fundamental to happiness at work.

As far as careers are concerned, it's impossible to make provision for everyone to progress, at least in the conventional sense. Not everyone can get the top job and the funnel narrows as you rise. But the PROGRESSIVE ORGANISATION, by its very nature, thinks of 'progress' as 'making things

---

11 Many experiments have confirmed this, including one where people are presented with the choice of having a large pay increase now, followed by three years of pay cuts, or a smaller increase now and three years of pay rises. People choose the latter even if the total sum earned is less.

12 M.J. Patterson, P.B. Warr and M.A. West, 'Organisational Climate and Company Productivity: The Role of Employee Affect and Employee Level', *Journal of Occupational and Organizational Psychology* 77(2) (2004), 193–216.

13 The actual figure was +0.74 (that's three-quarters of the way to a perfect correlation score of +1). A 'correlation' is a close relationship between two or more variables. A correlation of +1 means the relationship is as close as it possibly can be whereas a correlation of -1 means the two variables are working against each other to the greatest possible extent. A correlation of zero means there is no relationship.

better than they were before'. This is less about formal status and position than people's ability to make a contribution and be recognised for it. In organisations throughout the world there has been an explosion of grand-sounding job titles. This is a symptom of the fact that it's harder to make upward progress in flatter organisations. High-faluting titles,[14] rather than pay rises, are handed out to create an illusion of progress.

More pay may be seen as a sign of progress. But the link between pay and happiness is complicated. Researchers constantly find that although pay does not generate satisfaction, perceptions that it's too low can cause great dissatisfaction. After all, the pay you receive places a value on you and your skills. To assess if your pay is too low you'll compare sideways with others of similar standing inside and outside your organisation. Another problem is that as soon as you do get a pay rise it's psychologically absorbed. It doesn't provide a boost to happiness for very long. Even if you win the lottery, studies show that it takes about six months for the novelty to wear off. Yet, for all that, it is important to feel some progress is being made in pay. When economies are in recession and pay is held down, or goes backwards, it does have the effect of draining away some of people's happiness at work.

Comfort

At the base of Maslow's 'Model of Human Needs' are all those basic comforts humans need for survival, such as nutritious food and drink, physical security, enough sleep and an environment that doesn't cause you any harm. It's difficult, if not impossible, to be happy if you're working in conditions that are uncomfortable or worse. You would think that modern organisations are well past the point where such basic needs are a problem, wouldn't you? It appears not. In the next chapter I'll be looking in some detail at the way employees are harmed at work. As you'll see, there are plenty of ways employees suffer in poor working environments. Despite all the progress that has been made in health and safety at work in the last few decades, there is still much for PROGRESSIVE ORGANISATIONS to do.

Here's just one example – diet. In organisations where the pace of work is fast and furious many people don't eat properly. This can extend into the evening where there's no time or energy to do anything but eat convenience

---

14 This subject has a funny side. How about 'Director of First Impressions' (Receptionist) or 'Ambient Replenishment Controller' (shelf-stacker)?

foods stuffed with salt and sugar. The quality of diet has a major influence on physical and mental health.[15] The PROGRESSIVE ORGANISATION will tackle the subject of employees' dietary needs as an integral part of health and safety policy. Other areas constantly needing attention include lighting, air quality, temperature, atmospheric pollution, tool and equipment hazards, office layouts, standards of decoration, cleanliness, noise and vibration.

Surveys continue to show that improvements in physical working conditions contribute positively to employees' happiness and job satisfaction. Principled Persuasion's role in this area is to provide information to employees not just on the usual health and safety subjects, but also on a whole range of issues related to individuals' mental and physical health.

Job Satisfaction and Happiness

Employee attitude surveys regularly record job satisfaction levels of 80 per cent or more. What does this tell you? Can you conclude that the majority of people are happy at work? No you can't. The clue lies in the word 'job'. Job satisfaction is defined as a 'pleasurable emotional state resulting from the appraisal of one's job'.[16] Most people like doing their jobs. That's when they use their skills and become absorbed. You are in a very bad place indeed if you're not getting any satisfaction from the work itself, which, by the way, is usually the case for around a fifth of the workforce.

It's possible for people to be satisfied with their jobs and yet be unhappy at work, for example, because of the systems, management, culture or relationships they have with others. So while job satisfaction is a useful measure it should be seen as only one part of the story. Over the years numerous attempts have been made to link job satisfaction with organisational performance. The outcome of this research has been to establish correlations between job satisfaction and many different aspects of life at work.

Here are some examples:[17] (the correlations are expressed as percentages, so the way to read these figures is '82 per cent of job satisfaction is linked to acceptance by group members' and so on).

---

15 See Courtney van der Wayer, *Changing Diets, Changing Minds: How Food Affects Mental Well-Being and Behaviour* (Sustain, 2005).

16 E.A. Locke, 'What is Job Satisfaction?', *Organisational Behaviour and Human Performance* 4(4) (1969), 309–36.

17 These data come from a wide range of different surveys and are just some examples of the many components of job satisfaction.

Acceptance by group members	82%
Personal development opportunities	74%
Opportunities to acquire new skills	59%
Levels of performance feedback	57%
Autonomy	50%
Good use of skills	48%
Perception of good supervisory support	46%
Making friends at work	45%
Significance of task	38%
Level of income	25%

Overall it's been estimated that 30 per cent of the performance of an organisation is linked to the job satisfaction of employees.[18] Although job satisfaction has been a useful measure that approximates to employees' happiness at work, it's a relatively one-dimensional reading. When people agree in surveys they are 'satisfied with their jobs', they are likely to be thinking largely about the job itself, not everything that surrounds it. What's needed is a multi-dimensional picture of employees' happiness at work. Enter the Happiness Profile.

The Happiness Profile

The PROGRESSIVE ORGANISATION's Happiness Profile is based on the six sources of happiness. It allows you to calculate one overall combined statistic which will be a more accurate reflection of employees' levels of happiness. More importantly, it enables you to map out zones of strength and weakness throughout the organisation. The data for the Happiness Profile is drawn from both quantitative and qualitative feedback. This can take the form of answers to specific questions in surveys or from open-ended, unsought opinions flowing in from new channels of communication. Emotional and rational measures are included and differentiated. The latest analytic software is employed to cluster feedback into the six sources of happiness. The Happiness Profile needs constant updating to provide a running commentary on the organisation's ability to create a happy working environment.

Although every organisation has different characteristics, the six sources of happiness do not vary. They apply everywhere. So here's a simple model

---

18   T.A. Judge, C.J. Thoresen, J.E. Bono and G.K. Patton, 'The Job Satisfaction – Job Performance Relationship: A Qualitative and Quantitative Review', *Psychological Bulletin* 127(3) (2001), 376–407. The combined sample size was 54,417.

to help you begin the process of devising a Happiness Profile for your own organisation. Just six examples are given in each source – many more measures can be added into each box. What matters is that you produce a 'score' for each of your sources of happiness based on the feedback you receive.

LOVE	SELF-ESTEEM	CONTROL
• Warm relationships	• Respected	• Control over tasks
• Concern for your welfare	• Significance of job	• Free to make decisions
• Supportive supervision	• Contribute to decisions	• Freedom to initiate
• Acceptance	• Work recognised	• Mastery of skills
• Friendly co-operation	• Fairly treated	• Well informed
• Personal feedback	• Get ideas listened to	• Clear about future
PLEASURE	PROGRESS	COMFORT
• Variety of tasks	• Can grow and develop	• Enough breaks/rest
• New experiences	• Learning new things	• Hours worked OK
• Humour, banter	• Real advancement	• Good diet
• Using your skills	• Sense of achievement	• Comfortable workspace
• Creative opportunities	• Setting your own goals	• Feel physically secure
• Getting into flow	• Progressing financially	• Amenities good

The Happiness Profile is the first of three steps towards describing the organisation's culture in more depth than is possible with the conventional attitude survey. It uses a wider range of measures, both rational and emotional. It gathers information through more channels and uses more sophisticated analytical techniques to map out where the organisation is succeeding and failing. It provides the material for this major element of Principled Persuasion that's all about raising levels of happiness.

The Principles of Hedonic Persuasion

Although pleasure is just one of the six sources of happiness, I've chosen the word 'hedonic' because Principled Persuasion, in this context, is setting out to support an environment where employees can derive more pleasure from all aspects of their life at work. This is going to have to become a top priority in organisations. Employees are not inspired by the now dated concept of having 'job satisfaction'. They want to be happy and fulfilled at work. In the future, the best people will want to join PROGRESSIVE ORGANISATIONS where leaders understand work isn't just about making a living, but about living to the full. So here are the Principles of Hedonic Persuasion, the second of our seven sets of principles designed to change organisational cultures for the better.

Principle 1: Create the Happiness Profile

This allows you to see areas of strength and weakness for each of the six sources of happiness. Get started by using existing attitude surveys and cluster the responses into the six sources. Feed in the new data as they become available and employ the latest analytical techniques.

Principle 2: Explain why you want a happier organisation

None of this work should be going on mysteriously in the background. Be up front about it – tell employees what's going on and why it's such an important priority. Divide up the campaign content to reflect the six sources and open up the issues to fuel the organisation-wide conversation.

Principle 3: Cover rational and emotional dimensions

The Happiness Profile is the first step towards measuring the emotional climate of the organisation. This is new territory for many. It's essential to find out how people *feel* about themselves and others in the workplace.

Principle 4: Change the vocabulary of the organisation

This needs conscious effort. In developing communication material you should go out of your way to use the vocabulary of happiness. Good words will help to support good vibes. Construct your own carefully chosen word list using a dictionary and a thesaurus.

So now you're off and running. But at some point during this chapter you may well have said to yourself: 'this is all very well, but the real world of working life is harsh and difficult for many – happiness at work is a great ideal but not realisable'. Well, that's why the next subject needs to be covered. It's ignored by the vast majority of books on management and communication. It's the dark side of organisations – the harm that's experienced by so many employees during a normal working day.

CHAPTER 5

Harm at Work: The Principles of Mindful Persuasion

Out of the crooked timber of humanity no straight thing was ever made.[1]

Harm in organisations is corrosive. Unchecked, it seeps into every corner. Anyone who has worked in any organisation for any length of time has experienced it. Yet, outside of conventional health and safety issues, the subject is hardly covered in business books, with a few exceptions.[2] Why? Mainly because it's unpleasant to have to face up to the darker side of human nature; second, because data on harms at work are not yet being fully collected. But if Principled Persuaders are to have any chance of creating a happy working environment, they must be aware of the numerous harmful barriers in the way.

In the PROGRESSIVE ORGANISATION, Principled Persuaders will set themselves the objective of using communication to minimise harm, alongside that of maximising happiness. They will use new measures of harm, and capture them in a Harm Profile to put alongside the Happiness Profile. Tapping into three of the strategic drivers of change, EDUCATION, MENTALISATION and COMMUNICATION, they will use the principles of Mindful Persuasion, described at the end of this chapter, to make all employees more aware of the harms present in the organisation, and advise on how to deal with them.

My focus is on harms experienced by employees. Harms inflicted on customers, suppliers, the environment and local communities are outside the scope of this book, but these can also be considerable.

---

1   Immanuel Kant, *Idea for a General History with a Cosmopolitan Purpose* (1784), in Proposition Six.

2   For example, Adrian Furnham and John Taylor, *The Dark Side of Behaviour at Work* (Palgrave Macmillan, 2004) and Adrian Furnham and John Taylor, *Bad Apples* (Palgrave Macmillan, 2011).

How Organisations Harm Employees

Organisations have the potential to inflict enormous harms on their employees. Over the last century legislation has been put in place to reduce many harms, particularly those associated with working conditions. Yet even now, in the second decade of the twenty-first century, there is plenty of evidence of employees being physically harmed.

During 2012/13, 148 people were killed at work in Britain. Some 78,000 other injuries were reported and 1.1 million people were diagnosed as suffering with a work-related illness, resulting in 27 million working days being lost.[3] In 2013/14 there were 150 work-related fatalities and 12,000 early deaths due to poor working conditions in the past.[4] Each year, Britain's Health and Safety Executive calculates that the cost to the economy is in the region of £14 billion. If this is happening in Britain, where extreme care is taken over health and safety issues, think what must be happening in parts of the world where regulations and attitudes are far more lax.

Excessive working hours in pressurised conditions are another major source of harm to employees. American, Japanese and British organisations commonly have cultures where employees are expected to work long hours. In Britain, 11 per cent of all employees work between 49 and 60 hours per week. Many people work far longer than that, not to mention the additional strain of commuting and work in private time. The new mobile technologies aren't helping. They are being used in such a way that it's almost impossible for some employees to escape work. That's down to management culture. Organisations need to evolve protocols so that it becomes acceptable for employees to draw down the shutters on work-related mobile communications. Instead, it's apparent that many workaholic managers expect their staff to derive the same satisfaction from constant texts, emails and phone calls as they do.

How Employees Harm Organisations

Theft comes high on the list of harms caused by employees. By some estimates at least 5 per cent of employees steal in most work settings. Apparently, up to 50 per cent of employees will steal if they have access to cash and other valuables.[5] Fraud ranges from high-level deceptions to fiddling expenses.

3   Health & Safety Executive, *Annual Statistics Report for Great Britain 2012/13*, 1.
4   Health & Safety Executive, *Annual Statistics Report for Great Britain 2013/14*, 5.
5   Furnham and Taylor, *Bad Apples*, 21.

Corrupt practices such as bribes and kickbacks, now being cracked down on through legislation,[6] used to be commonplace. Other categories of harm that have direct costs for organisations include vandalism, sabotage and the deliberate waste of resources.

There are many ways to evade work, including throwing 'sickies', coming in late regularly, skiving off early, working slowly and pretending to work.[7] People who come to work stuffed with drugs or alcohol can't operate efficiently. Everyone occasionally needs to carry out a private task in work time, but there are those who make a habit of it. An organisation's reputation can be badly damaged by employees spreading false rumours, behaving badly with customers, or passing confidential information to competitors and the media.

How Employees Harm Other Employees

Bullying has been called a 'silent epidemic'. According to the Chartered Institute of Personnel Development (CIPD) it costs UK employers over £2 billion every year. Typical bullying behaviours include verbal abuse, undermining and belittling, rudeness and foul language, unfair punishments, constant criticism, mental and physical intimidation, physical abuse and other forms of victimisation. The CIPD issued a guidance paper on bullying[8] that noted despite the fact the vast majority of organisations have anti-bullying policies, the incidence of bullying remains high. Studies reveal that up to a third of workers in some organisations have been bullied, in some cases for longer than a year.

Other ways of employees being nasty to each other include verbal and sexual harassment, constant disturbance and favouritism. Some managers take their subordinates' work and claim it for their own. Others put excessive pressure on their teams to work harder, faster, for longer. There are acts of omission such as not putting someone forward for training, more pay or promotion when they deserve it. In the area of communication there are all kinds of harmful behaviours such as misinforming, deceiving, lying and failing to keep people informed about important matters that affect them.

---

6   The UK Bribery Act of 2011.
7   I remember one person who regularly used to leave his jacket on the back of the chair, pens and papers scattered across the desk, to make it look as if he was still working when in fact he'd gone home early.
8   Chartered Institute of Personnel Development, *Bullying at Work: Beyond Policies to a Culture of Respect* (2013), 3.

Vulnerable People

Some employees are more vulnerable than others. If bullying is a silent epidemic, then poor mental health at work is the problem that dares not speak its name. According to a paper produced by the Sainsbury Centre for Mental Health:[9] 'At any one time, one worker in six will be experiencing depression, anxiety, or problems related to stress'. If alcohol or drug dependency is included, this figure rises to 20 per cent of all employees in Britain. The Health and Safety Executive records that over 200,000 new cases of stress, depression and anxiety are reported every year, with each case involving 24 lost working days on average.[10] A 2014 survey by Friends Life found 40 per cent of employees experienced a common mental health problem over the last year but said nothing about it to their boss for fear of it affecting their career prospects.

Why should this come as a surprise? After all, nearly 30 per cent of the British population have, at some time in their lives, been diagnosed with a mental health problem. Yet, the same Sainsbury paper reported that nearly half of all employers thought that none of their workers would suffer mental health problems during their working life. What an astonishing finding! If any proof was needed of the absolute necessity of tackling this subject in organisations, this is it. Anyone who continues to doubt that there is a need for more empathy with vulnerable people should read a January 2014 report from the National Council for Palliative Care. This found that 32 per cent of employees bereaved in the past five years felt that their employers had not treated them with compassion.

Harmful Thoughts

You don't need to be diagnosed with a mental illness to suffer from harmful mental habits. Even the healthiest mind has a wonderful capacity for getting its thinking in a twist. This has been spelt out in no uncertain terms by psychologists like Daniel Kahneman.[11] He says there are two 'systems of thought': one is fast and immediate like a set of mental reflexes; the other is more considered and calculated. Guess which one you use the vast majority of the time? Using mental shortcuts you oversimplify, employ

---

9   The Sainsbury Centre for Mental Health, *Mental Health at Work: Developing the Business Case*, Policy Paper 8 (2013), 1.
10   Health & Safety Executive, *Annual Statistics Report for Great Britain 2012/13*, 7.
11   Daniel Kahneman, *Thinking Fast and Slow* (Penguin, 2012).

stereotypes to make hasty judgements, jump to conclusions, see causes and intentions where none exist, think you understand when you don't. What's more, you're useless at assessing risk and probabilities, rare events figure disproportionately in your calculations and you suffer more from your losses than you enjoy your gains. You're easily 'primed', which means your responses are conditioned by stimuli of which you're totally unaware. You misremember things and you're subject to illusions, one of which is that you're overconfident about your own abilities; everyone thinks they're better than average, which just isn't possible.

And all that muddled thinking is taking place on a normal working day. If that wasn't bad enough, clinical psychologists have plenty of evidence to show how prone you are to 'cognitive distortions'. Here are some examples:[12] see if you recognise them.

All or nothing thinking	*Either I'm a success or failure*
Mental filter	*I made a mistake so everything I do is wrong*
Over-generalisation	*I failed that exam so I'll never be any good at that subject*
Magnification	*He says he didn't like me so he must hate me*
Minimisation	*She said she likes me but probably doesn't mean it*
Personalisation	*He looks angry so he must be angry with me*
Emotional reasoning	*I feel the future is black so it must be hopeless*
Discounting positives	*I managed to do that, but I was only lucky*
Mind reading	*Her silence means she doesn't like me*
Fortune telling	*I am not going to enjoy that event*
Catastrophising	*My heart's beating fast – a heart attack's on the way*
Labelling	*I didn't just make a mistake – I proved I'm a fool*

One broad category of harmful thinking that causes a great deal of trouble is self-deception. You have your way of looking at the world (your 'schema') and you persuade yourself that it's the right way. It's a small step from there to converting your vices into virtues. The bully convinces himself he's just being firm, or not suffering fools gladly. The liar tells herself it's none of their business

---

12 Adapted from Alan Carr and Muireann McNulty (eds), *The Handbook of Adult Clinical Psychology* (2006), 69.

anyway. Managers, inflicting heavy workloads on staff, tell themselves it's the only way to stay ahead of the game.

It seems to be inevitable that, as we go through the working day, our minds fill up with harmful thoughts even if we don't recognise them as such. In many situations reflexive, distorted and self-deceiving thoughts won't have any serious consequences, but in organisations they lead to bad decisions, poor relationships and failures of leadership. Discussion, conversation, debate and challenge, stimulated by Principled Persuaders, are the best antidotes to the poison of harmful thoughts.

Harmful Emotions

Then there's the little problem of emotions. There was a time when conscious efforts were made to eliminate emotions from the workplace. It was the sociologist Max Weber who said:

> the more the bureaucracy is 'dehumanised' the more completely it succeeds in eliminating from official business love, hatred and all purely personal, irrational and emotional elements which escape calculation. This is the specific nature of bureaucracy and it is apprised as its special value.[13]

Despite the fact that most organisations are moving gradually from a bureaucratic model to a participative one, there are still plenty of managers who would agree with Weber. Unfortunately for them, emotions can't be taken out of working life. As I pointed out in Chapter 3, they play an entirely reasonable part in guiding decisions and actions.

Yet, as everyone knows, there is an immensely harmful side to emotions too. They can stimulate specifically bad acts. For example, resentment might prompt someone to steal, jealousy can lead to co-operation being withheld, anger might result in aggression. Someone deeply hurt may turn to acts of revenge. Anyone can be affected in this way:

> almost anyone in the organisation is a potential threat, in the sense that things can happen to people in and outside the organisation

---

13 Max Weber, *Essays in Sociology* (Oxford University Press, 1946). Also quoted in Roy Payne and Cary Cooper, *Emotions at Work* (John Wiley & Sons, 2009), 219.

to change a conscientious, moral and trustworthy individual into a
serious threat to the welfare of the organisation.[14]

Bad conditions, bad environments, bad actions on the part of managers, all spark bad behaviour from otherwise good people.

Psychologists[15] have identified ten basic emotional ranges. When you list them, you can't help noticing that most of them are negative.

- Interest – excitement
- Enjoyment – joy
- Startle – surprise
- Distress – anguish
- Rage – anger
- Disgust – revulsion
- Contempt – scorn
- Fear – terror
- Shame – shyness – humiliation
- Guilt – remorse

Like an artist's palette of colours, these emotions are mingled and mixed with each other to create an endless variety of feelings. The sheer complexity and changeability of emotions would seem to make management of them a hopeless task. That's why organisations need to create an environment in which employees are better able to manage their own emotions. They should be educated and supported, through Principled Persuasion, to express their emotions and treat them as guides to what they feel is right or wrong in particular situations. Line managers should be trained to recognise emotions during conversations and by watching body language.

In the PROGRESSIVE ORGANISATION the opportunity to open up to others and say what you feel will provide release and help to move things on without negative consequences. Emotional issues will be discussed and understood as part of the normal process of continuous improvement and culture change. If this can be done, an enormous amount of pressure will be released to the benefit of everyone. Well, perhaps not everyone. After all, there is, in every organisation of any size, a number of bad people that can thrive in harmful conditions.

---

14 Furnham and Taylor, *Bad Apples*, 216.
15 See the discussion in Chaper 1 of Payne and Cooper, *Emotions at Work*, 3–19.

Bad People

They don't have to be many in number. Like yeast in a barrel bad people are capable of fermenting an amount of harm that's disproportionate to their numbers. It's possible some of them are right at the top. It's not only thieves and fraudsters you have to worry about, it's certain personality types. Let's focus on just two of them – narcissists and psychopaths. See if you recognise anybody.

About one in a hundred people is a narcissist. Narcissists[16] are hopelessly in love with themselves; they think they are just great at everything they do and won't accept any criticism to the contrary. If challenged, they are likely to respond aggressively since their whole worldview is centred on their superiority. That's why they're happy to exploit others who they see as beneath them. They have an inflated sense of their own importance. They are suspicious of others and devalue them, unconcerned about any damage this might do. They are good at organisational politics, projecting high levels of confidence that can be mistaken for competence.

If you have a boss like this, it's a mistake to tell him how you feel. He won't have any empathy. You should avoid conflict, get written instructions for your work if possible, and keep records. If you want to get on with him, give him credit for your accomplishments. If you suspect any of your peer group are narcissists, watch your back and don't reveal your vulnerabilities or they will make use of them. If you share your good ideas with them expect them to take them upstairs and claim them for their own. You can see narcissism at work in the smugness of people who think they're right all the time, in the stupidity of prejudice and in the shallow search for social prestige.

Then there are the corporate psychopaths, or 'snakes in suits'.[17]

Although they look normal, they are very much not normal. Psychopaths exhibit a wide range of characteristics including a complete lack of empathy with others, remorselessness, deceit, grandiosity, impulsiveness, irresponsibility, disregard for safety, irritability and aggression. Yet they are not easy to spot. Far from it. They are masters of 'impression management', changing their character depending on who they're with, flattering bosses while cruel to subordinates. Not merely two-faced, they have multiple masks.

Psychologist Paul Babiak, who's made a special study of this species, believes 'most of us will come across at least one psychopath during a typical

---

16 In the Greek myth, Narcissus starved to death unable to stop admiring his own reflection in a crystal pool.
17 Paul Babiak and Robert D. Hare, *Snakes in Suits: When Psychopaths Go to Work* (Regan Books, 2006).

day'.[18] These people can be superficially charming. They are fond of using jargon and clichés, concealing their lack of substance behind management-speak. They thrive in fast moving, high-risk work cultures, particularly when their organisations have inconsistent or fuzzy policies that allow people to get away with bad behaviour. Although they are poor team players and leave a string of damaged relationships in their wake, the glibness and fearlessness of psychopaths can be useful assets in some organisational cultures. The consequences of letting them loose in senior positions can be terrible. The events of 2008, when financial markets and businesses came crashing down, have been described as a 'mass outbreak of corporate psychopathy'.[19]

As with narcissists, around 1 per cent of the general population is psychopathic. Another 10 per cent of the population fall in the 'grey zone', not completely psychopathic but behaving in a way that causes concerns to others. Many psychopaths are in prison, but there are plenty of them thriving in organisations. Using original research Babiak and Hare estimated that around 3.5 per cent of the high-flying executives they studied fitted the psychopathic profile.

There will always be bad people in organisations. You can try to screen them out but you can't always spot the lies. At minimum, around 15 per cent of all CVs contain lies and distortions. Some people are good at 'gaming' psychometric and other tests. The only way of minimising the harm they do is to create a culture in which they stand out and are more easily recognised. That's where Principled Persuasion comes in. Its role is to educate and make people more aware of the types of behaviour to watch out for. There need to be more channels of face-to-face communication where employees can report their concerns confidentially and be taken seriously. Above all, the culture should be one where it's clear that 'you don't have to put up with this behaviour'.

Bad Company

Crowds can bring out the worst in people. So can groups. Fortunately, crowd behaviour in organisations is not as common now as it used to be, though mass meetings and protests still take place. It seems that people jettison their individuality when they become part of a crowd. Gustav Le Bon was one of the first to notice the curious effect that being part of a crowd has on individuals. He

---

18 Babiak and Hare, *Snakes in Suits*, 37.
19 Remark made by Dr Oliver James in a TV programme called *Psychopath-night* broadcast by Channel 4 in December 2013.

said that crowds have 'a collective mind which makes them feel, think and act in a manner quite different from that in which each individual of them would feel, think and act were he in a state of isolation'.[20] When you join a crowd, it's easy to become swept along in its emotions. Le Bon called this 'emotional contagion' and modern psychologists refer to it as a 'psychological epidemic'. In the early twentieth century, Carl Jung warned that:

> Man in the mass sinks unconsciously to an inferior, moral and intellectual level, to that level which is always there, below the threshold of consciousness, ready to break forth as soon as it is activated by the formation of a mass.[21]

But if crowds are less common in organisations, groups are everywhere. Does belonging to a group have a similar effect to being part of a crowd? The answer, broadly, is yes, it can do. There are lots of downsides to group behaviour. The natural tendency to want to 'fit in' can lead to 'groupthink', a term invented in the early 1970s by Irving Janis, a research psychologist at Yale. Individuals prefer to join a consensus rather than argue from a different position. This is a harmful habit since often what's needed is vigorous debate, not comfortable agreement. In groups of more than 12 people there's a tendency for 'social loafing' to cut in: some members of the group sit back and let the others get on with it.

Groups can become set in their ways. Group members can start to reinforce each other's views and, in the worst cases, this leads to prejudice and closed minds. Shared emotions in the group may generate hostile feelings towards other groups, particularly if they think their values are being challenged. You can end up with 'a dysfunctional corporate culture in which the big established groups are allowed to prey upon emerging teams, belittle their efforts, and over time, hector them out of existence'.[22] One reason why it can be so difficult to change cultures after a takeover or merger is that people fiercely defend group identities. Once groups start to set themselves apart they can start to think that they're better than others. Silos and cliques form. Sharing suffers. Communication dries up.

---

20 Gustav Le Bon, *The Crowd: A Study of the Popular Mind* (Ernest Benn, 1947 [1896]), 27.
21 From the collected works of C.J. Jung quoted in Steven Bartlett, *The Pathology of Man: A Study of Human Evil* (Charles C. Thomas, 2005), 97.
22 From Dick Brass, 'Microsoft's Creative Destruction', *New York Times*, 4 February 2010, A27, quoted in Edmund Phelps, *Mass Flourishing* (Princeton University Press, 2013), 242.

Groups are a necessary part of organisational life. To avoid the downsides of group behaviour, the PROGRESSIVE ORGANISATION encourages interconnection between different groups, injects new blood into long established groups, and keeps a wary eye open for groups that need to be broken up. As far as larger groups like departments are concerned, Principled Persuaders ensure they are kept well informed about other people's work, describing how everyone contributes to the common good.

Kicking Out Conformity

While engineered organisations can encourage conformity, PROGRESSIVE ORGANISATIONS aim to kick it out. That's not to say they want constant disorder or rebellion but they understand that the human tendency to conform is the opposite of independent thinking and creativity. Conforming slips easily into compliance and unthinking obedience. That's what happened when Stanley Milgram conducted his experiments.[23]

Milgram was intrigued by the fact that so many civilians had taken part in the mass killings of men, women and children during the Holocaust. He recruited members of the public to take part in a 'learning' experiment. These men (they were all men) were told their task was to teach a 'learner' (an actor) who they could see sitting in a chair wired up to an electric current. An authority figure ordered them to apply an electric shock every time the learner failed to answer a question correctly. While the shocks were being applied at increasing intensity, the teachers were told it was fine to carry on, despite the fact they could see the learner exhibiting signs of great pain, and then appearing to pass out. Sixty-five per cent of the men who took part were prepared to apply a lethal dose of 450 volts. One of the most disturbing aspects of the experiments was the way these ordinary men, 'off the street', turned into killing machines. Milgram described a teacher's 'hard impassive face, showing total indifference as he subdues the screaming learner'.

Research after the Second World War found that the characteristics of those who refused to take part in Nazi killings were independent thought, emotional self-reliance, refusal to conform, comply or be apathetic, a capacity for empathy and a high level of moral sensibility.[24] It would be hard to find better descriptors for the ideal employee in the PROGRESSIVE ORGANISATION.

23 The experiments started in 1961 and the results were published in Stanley Milgram, *Obedience to Authority: An Experimental View* (Tavistock, 1974).
24 Bartlett, *The Pathology of Man*, 182.

Harming Others Can Be Fun

If you've ever puzzled over how it is that some people can be so nasty towards others, puzzle no more. All the evidence shows that people derive all kinds of emotional benefits from harming others. Sigmund Freud believed that 'people habitually permit themselves to do any bad deed that procures them something they want, if only they are sure that no authority will discover it or make them suffer for it'.[25] There are strong emotional incentives to harm. Consider the pleasures to be derived from hatred, for example.

Hatred is a destructive force. Its aim is to eliminate the hated object. This can be an individual, a group or even a whole nation. Hatred can stem from anxiety, fear, or the feeling that your interests are being damaged. The fact that other people are different from you can take you along the path from mistrust, to dislike and then to hatred. It's an intense emotion and therein lies one of its main benefits – hatred can make life seem more exciting. Hatred simplifies reality, strengthens self-identity, provides emotional security, increases the hater's sense of power and makes him feel more alert and alive. It's a paradox that hateful, murderous terrorists show themselves capable of dedication, courage, strong social purpose and moral superiority.

Bearing this in mind, it's easy to see how warfare can be enjoyable for certain individuals, especially in organisations. Just look at the kind of political in-fighting that breaks out as rivals seek to kill off each other's careers. Here's Freud again:

> Work is no less valuable for the opportunity it, and the human relations connected with it, provide for a very considerable discharge of libidinal component impulses, narcissistic, aggressive and even erotic.[26]

He added: 'homo homini lupus' (man is wolf to man). Work environments give human wolves the perfect territory in which to find their prey. In private life you can walk away from people that you think might harm you, at work you don't always have that choice.

Another source of harm that brings people joy is prejudice. A great deal of work has taken place in organisations to minimise prejudice. In the 1970s prejudices against minority groups were commonplace. At that time, black

---

25   Sigmund Freud, *Civilisation and its Discontents*, trans. Joan Riviere (Hogarth Press, 1930), 107.
26   Freud, *Civilisation*, 34.

people, gays, the disabled and the mentally ill were all 'fair game' for jokes and discrimination. Male managers were prejudiced about the roles they thought women could play in organisations. One of the great joys of prejudice is that it simplifies the world enormously. Elisabeth Young-Bruehl says that in the world of prejudice 'people and things have well-known places, and do expected things. We feel at home there. We fit in. We are members. We know the way around'.[27] Like hatred, prejudice brings strengthened self-identity, a sense of self-satisfaction and power. You know you are right and they are wrong. History tells us prejudice and persecution are bedfellows.

Towards a Harm Profile

Nobel prize-winning psychologist, Daniel Kahneman, thinks that 'It is now conceivable, as it was not even a few years ago, that an index of the amount of suffering in society will someday be included in national statistics'.[28] The same principle applies to organisations. Most well run organisations already collect a lot of information that can contribute to the new concept of a 'Harm Profile'. Even so, far more data can be pulled together to give a more accurate picture of the dark side of the organisation. The purpose of the 'Harm Profile' is to give senior management and Principled Persuaders a realistic fix on the barriers to creating a happy working environment.

This is new territory. It means gathering up all the health and safety statistics and bringing them alongside a range of other measures. Here are some examples: acts that break the law or important regulations such as fraud, theft, sabotage and vandalism; interpersonal harms such as incidents of bullying, sexual harassment, violence, aggressive behaviour and verbal abuse; reports of alcohol and drug abuse, regular late attendance and reasons for dismissals. Channels of communication for whistle-blowing and internal complaints will bring in more information. Counselling services for stress and other personal problems would enable the organisation to be more clear-eyed about the mental health of its workforce.

Most organisations are a long way off from being able to compile a comprehensive database of issues related to harm. What's needed is a mindset on the part of senior managers that recognises the harmful and costly nature of the dark side of work, and a culture that encourages open dialogue. With their

27   Elisabeth Young-Bruehl, *The Anatomy of Prejudices* (Harvard University Press, 1996), 192.
28   Kahneman, *Thinking Fast and Slow*, 410.

support, Principled Persuaders can get to work, using 'Mindful Persuasion' to help minimise harms.

The Principles of Mindful Persuasion

Why 'mindful'? Mindfulness is all about being more aware of your own mental states and those of the people around you. It's about giving more consideration to your own thoughts and feelings and those of others. It's about increasing attentiveness to what's going on in the present moment and using that greater awareness to improve relationships. Persuasion has a major role to play in this context. The principles that follow will help you create appropriate material.

> **Principle 1: Build a Harm Profile**
> Even if it can't be complete to begin with, it's important to have a better picture of the dark side of the organisation. Then you can begin to identify the main problem areas and make plans for minimising their impact.
>
> **Principle 2: Describe the different types of harm that are present in the organisation**
> Be open about this. It's the first stage in creating awareness of the problems that need to be fixed. Provide information on the resources available to help employees counter harmful experiences. Make it clear what the policies are across the wide range of potential harms.
>
> **Principle 3: Highlight unacceptable behaviours**
> Explain how people are expected to behave towards one another. Make clear what people need to do if faced by bad behaviour. Use powerful emotional language to help create a sense of shame in those who are behaving badly.
>
> **Principle 4: Encourage a sense of personal responsibility towards minimising harms**
> Tell employees that if they don't think something is right they should be prepared to challenge it: that if they slavishly follow commands, even if they know harms will result, they have jettisoned their moral responsibility; that passivity is the same as complicity.

The costs of harm at work are high. Who pays them? The organisation pays in terms of reduced performance as well as fines. The state pays for health services that have to cope with the physical and psychological harms experienced by employees as a result of their work. However, in the end it's employees themselves that pay the greatest price in terms of stress, strain, impact on family and social life and shorter life spans.

Equipped with the Happiness Profile and the Harm Profile, Principled Persuaders are now in a better position to develop a wide range of material focused on maximising employees' happiness and minimising the harm that comes to them. But there's still something missing. To give additional shape and strength to Principled Persuasion, there's a need to bind it into a clear and meaningful ethical framework.

CHAPTER 6

The Good Life at Work: The Principles of Ethical Persuasion

Just improve yourself. That's all you can do to improve the world.[1]

What does it mean to live 'a good life' at work? It means being happy, certainly. And free from as many harms as possible. It also means having the opportunity to develop as an individual – to grow, to flourish in body and mind. None of this is possible unless the organisation is ethical through and through. In the twenty-first century, with increasingly educated, worldly-wise employees from diverse backgrounds, a living, breathing ethical culture, nurtured by Principled Persuasion, will be essential to innovation and advances in productivity.

From early times, accepted norms on how people should behave towards each other, have allowed human societies to hold themselves together, and sometimes make progress. These norms keep changing and will continue to do so in response to social and technological innovations. Yet, at root, there are a small number of universal principles that have emerged over centuries of discussion about ethics. How can they be identified?

The task set for this chapter is to go on a short tour of ethical theories; just enough for you to see how universal principles can be distilled out of the many different approaches taken to ethics over the centuries. The tour is chronological and has 12 stops. After each stop a specific lesson will be learned. The 12 lessons will then be distilled further into four ethical principles that form the foundations of the Principles of Ethical Persuasion.

Ethics are high on the agenda of many organisations today. In the past decade there has been a flurry of activity in this area, driven by legislation and punishments, including large fines, for unethical behaviour. In the UK the Bribery Act of 2011 provided further impetus. Sixty-six per cent of respondents

---

1   Ludwig Wittgenstein's advice to his friends, quoted in Ray Monk's biography, *The Duty of Genius* (Vintage, 1990), 17.

in a 2012 survey[2] said that issues of right and wrong are discussed in staff meetings. A 2013 survey[3] found 58 per cent of respondents thought their organisations were 'very ethical' or 'ethical'.

Yet, as far as employees are concerned, there's always the danger that ethics will become just another set of codes or instructions to be handed out to all new employees, another unread Bible kept in the back of the drawer. That's why ethics needs to be integrated into all forms of communication at work. It needs to be a high visibility subject. Employees need to learn more about ethics and engage in continuous discussion on the ethical behaviour (or not) they see around them.

Just one caveat before your tour begins. In attempting this little journey I take inspiration from one of the greatest thinkers of all time. During a public discussion in Oxford, Wittgenstein interrupted a speaker who had realised that he was about to say something that, although it was compelling, was clearly an oversimplification. He was trying to say something more sensible. 'No'. said Wittgenstein. 'Say what you have to say. Be crude and then we shall get on'.

Might is Right

This story of Western ethics begins around 3,000 years ago, in the age of the Greek Gods. They were a pretty immoral lot. Above ordinary mortals in every way, they did as they pleased. Ambitious humans aspired to be as godlike as possible. This was the age of the hero when the strongest, cleverest, craftiest men could rise to godlike status; like Achilles in the *Iliad* – passionate, bloodthirsty, proud; or Odysseus in the *Odyssey* – cunning, patient, resilient in the extreme. This was a time when might was right:

> *when the life of mankind was without order and like the life of beasts subject to the rule of strength, and there was no reward for the good nor any punishment of evil men.*[4]

The idea of laws, conventions and morals as a way of curbing violent men was by no means universally agreed as the way forward. In Plato's 'Gorgias', the

---

2   Sabrina Basran and Simon Webley, *Employee Views of Ethics at Work* (Institute of Business Ethics, 2012), 18.

3   Institute of Internal Communication, Ethics Survey (2013).

4   The quotation comes from a fragment of a Sisyphus play attributed to either Euripides or Critias the Tyrant written sometime in the fifth century BC.

politician Callicles argues that natural justice means strong men should rule over the weak and claim for themselves a greater share of wealth and power:

> In my opinion it's the weaklings who constitute the majority of the human race who make the rules ... They try to cow the stronger ones ... and to stop them getting an increased share by saying that to do so is wrong and comtemptible.

Lesson I: the physically and mentally strong will dominate the world if they are allowed to. However, in this context 'strong' is not really the right word. Maybe violent, authoritarian, egocentric or even psychopathic would be better words for those who wish to dominate. This applies in the workplace as much as anywhere else.

A Better Way to Live

By around the fifth century BC some thinkers were beginning to put forward ideas for a better way of life. Heraclitus believed that: 'Sound thinking is the greatest excellence and wisdom; to speak the truth and act according to nature, knowingly'.[5] Socrates taught his contemporaries to keep asking the right questions, test assumptions and challenge accepted views. He thought knowledge should be used in a practical way as a tool of discussion. It was important to share knowledge and be prepared to modify beliefs based on persuasive arguments and new information. From these discussions the best possible set of agreements will emerge. What a wonderful prescription for the modern knowledge economy!

In 'Nichomachean Ethics'[6] Aristotle says ethical understanding is the way to a happy and flourishing life. Although for him the highest form of happiness ('eudaimonia') is based on a life of wise, knowledgeable contemplation, he was reassuringly practical in his approach to day-to-day ethical behaviour. He saw practical wisdom as the process of understanding oneself and others. Morality was the means by which reason controls appetites and desires. For Aristotle, the practice of ethics was about getting into the right habits.

---

5   Charles H. Kahn, *Presocratic Greek Ethics: A History of Western Ethics*, edited by Lawrence C. Becker and Charlotte B. Becker (Routledge, 2003), 3.

6   So called because it is believed to have been edited by his son, Nichomachus. The ethical texts of Aristotle that we rely on were collected and edited in Rome in the first century BC by Andronicus of Rhodes.

> **Lesson 2**: the counterbalance to 'might is right' is the use of reason, by reasonable people, to work out the best practical way forward to live a better life. Reason is articulated through questioning, discussion and persuasive arguments.

Control Yourself

The idea that it is important to take responsibility for your own personal code of ethics was central to two very different ways of thinking about how to live a good life, Stoicism and Epicureanism.

The early Stoics believed that the world is part of a well-ordered universe in which a superhuman intelligence has designed everything for the best. The key for them to a smoothly flowing life was to look clearly at the world as it is, with all its goods and harms, and understand that some things are in your control and many are not. What you do need to control are your emotions. The concept of 'apatheia' (apathy) entails ridding yourself of emotions so completely that nothing can touch you, including the death of loved ones. The essence of Stoicism is self-analysis, self-understanding, self-control and a realistic view of what's possible to achieve in life.

Epicurus also advocated a clear-headed, self-analytical way of life. He told his disciples that God has delegated the running of the world to the laws of nature and that the time after death is no more worth worrying about than the time before birth. He urged them to concern themselves with maximising pleasure and minimising pain as the formula for a happy and good life. He reminded them that absence of pain is a pleasure and that a lot of pain derives from wanting something you can't have.

> **Lesson 3**: taking control over your thoughts and emotions is a central recurring theme of Western ethics. With increased freedoms comes a higher level of personal responsibility to act in ways that maximise happiness and minimise harms. This involves learning about, and using, what Michel Foucault called 'technologies of the self'.

From Good to God

From the birth of Christ until the twentieth century, ethical thinking in the Western world has been dominated by the concept of an all-seeing God. For roughly the first 1,500 years of this period, the doctrines of the Catholic church created a worldview of immense psychological power.

All humans, it taught, are fallen, miserable creatures[7] who are inherently sinful; 'inherently' because all are scarred by Adam's terrible mistake. Your life is a journey of suffering and repentance, a struggle to return to your former blissful state. However, this state is not achievable on earth – true happiness is only possible in heaven. All you can do while you're here on earth is submit with patience to suffering, be content with whatever hand God has given you to play, and obey the teachings of the church. The Catholic church developed a highly sophisticated framework of codes, backed by a penitential system. The codes included the Ten Commandments,[8] the Beatitudes[9] and the Catechism.[10] The penitential system worked on the basis that an all-seeing God knows what you are up to. Even if you escape punishment on earth, you'll suffer in hell for eternity unless you repent.

From the sixteenth century onwards the Protestant Reformation sent Christian ethics in a totally different direction. Luther set the ball rolling by arguing that faith delivers mankind from original sin and that, providing you follow your conscience, earthly happiness is consistent with a faithful life. Suffering is not an end in itself. God wants you to be happy. The ball was picked up by Jean Calvin who believed God had already picked him to go to heaven. Calvin saw himself as one of the 'elected'. But how could you tell the 'elected' from everyone else? One way, they decided, was by engaging successfully in the work of the world. Material gains, earned in the cut and thrust of competition, became an outward sign of inward blessedness. This idea that, in Max Weber's words, 'stood at the cradle of modern economic man'[11] provided the strongest possible justification for worldly success. Unlike Catholics, Calvinists believed that good works were not the way to get into heaven, but the sign you had already made it.

---

7   This wasn't a completely new idea. In the middle of the fifth century BC, in the 'Purification' of Empedocles, the human condition is pictured as a fall into misery from a primeval state of bliss.

8   Including 'don't kill, don't commit adultery, don't steal, don't lie'.

9   Amongst those blessed are 'those who mourn, the meek, the merciful, the peacemakers, the persecuted'.

10   The Catechism, whose origins go back to the early days of the church, is now a very detailed summary of the fundamental beliefs of Christian doctrine including the articles of faith, the sacraments, a section on the life of faith that deals with right conduct, and the role of prayer.

11   Max Weber, *The Protestant Ethic and the Spirit of Capitalism* [1905], translated by Talcott Parsons [1930] (Unwin, 1985), 174.

> **Lesson 4**: religious belief can be a powerful force for policing behaviour, with its system of eternal rewards and punishments. Yet history tells us that ethics based on religious beliefs need to be handled carefully. They can explode suddenly and destructively. Religion-based ethics have often been drowned in seas of blood.

The Ethics Inside You

By the seventeenth and eighteenth centuries some people were beginning to think hard about whether it would be possible to construct a meaningful system of ethics that relied less on God and more on humanity itself. The central question was: if there is no God to give you rules to obey, what's to stop you from becoming a dissolute pleasure-seeker, caring for no one but yourself? There was no rush to the exit marked 'atheist'. The vast majority of thinkers still believed in God. But there was a new attempt to reassert man's dignity as a rational creature, able to work things out for himself.

Thomas Hobbes[12] reminded his readers what things were like in a state of nature – lives were 'solitary, poor, nasty, brutish and short'.[13] People are selfish, he said, and can convince themselves of almost anything. They are natural predators so moral laws need to evolve, without any help from God, to ensure that we can protect ourselves from each other. These moral laws are natural laws that evolved long before societies were formed. He expressed one of the most important principles underlying ethical behaviour as follows:

> *Ignorance of the law of nature excuseth no man; because every man that has attained to the use of reason, is supposed to know, he ought not to do to another, what he would not have done to himself.*[14]

John Locke, who became a presiding spirit of the Enlightenment[15] in Britain, disagreed that there was any such thing as innate moral laws. In his *Essay*

---

12 In his masterwork *Leviathan*, published in London in 1651.
13 Thomas Hobbes, *Leviathan* (Oxford World Classics, 1998 [1651]), Part 1, Chapter 13, 9, 84.
14 Hobbes, *Leviathan*, Part 2, Chapter 27, 4, 194.
15 Defined roughly as the years between 1675 and 1800, the 'Enlightenment' was a period of intellectual revolution in Britain, part of a wider European phenomenon. Key to understanding the concept of 'Enlightenment' is the contrast between an age dominated by irrationality and superstition and one where the use of reason becomes the hallmark of a more mature society. The belief in progress was central to this 'age of reason'.

Concerning Human Understanding (1690) he pointed to the extraordinarily different cultures that existed around the world. He saw them as evidence that beliefs you think might be an essential part of human nature are nothing of the sort. Take attitudes to children for example. You might think it's natural to care for them, but other cultures, like the Mingrelians, seem happy to bury them alive.[16] Locke concluded that, when we're born, our minds are like a blank sheet of paper waiting for experience to write on it. That means no original sin. No one is condemned to be sinful. Reason gives us the power to build our own codes of ethical behaviour. But on what basis can you do this? According to Locke, it's the motivating principle of seeking pleasure and avoiding pain that is the foundation of morality: 'Things then are only good or evil in reference to pleasure and pain'.[17]

Lesson 5: it is up to people to agree amongst themselves what constitutes ethical behaviour. Listen to your inner voice telling you what is the right and most pleasant way to behave.

Motivations

What drives you to be good or evil? Hobbes said 'do unto others as you would be done by' and Locke, follow pleasure and avoid pain. But life's more complicated than that. There are all kinds of other motivations to act in one way or another.

Richard Cumberland said you are happiest when you're making other people happy. The Earl of Shaftesbury suggested you should act in accordance with the virtues you know to be good and then you'll feel good about yourself. Frances Hutcheson, Adam Smith's tutor, developed the concept of 'moral sense' and thought benevolence was the most motivating virtue.

In 1714, out of left field, came a provocative work that got conventional moralists buzzing with indignation. Bernard Mandeville[18] said it's vice not virtue that makes the world go round. Deep down you're driven by your desires for food, sex and luxuries of every kind. He argued that the economy depended

---

16 Locke lets himself go on this point: 'It is familiar among the Mingrelians, a people professing Christianity, to bury their children alive without scruple. There are places where they eat their own children. The Caribbs were wont to geld their children on purpose to fat and eat them'. *Essay Concerning Human Understanding* (Ward, Lock & Co., 1900 [1689]), Book 1, Chapter 3, 9, 31–2.

17 Locke, *Essay*, Book 2, Chapter 20, 2, 160.

18 Bernard Mandeville, *Fable of the Bees: or Private Vices, Public Benefits* (1714).

on self-interested vice. If we all abstained from our desires, trade would dry up, people would sit shivering in their houses.

David Hume took on the establishment with a secular view of ethics. He taught you should rely on your emotions as motivating forces rather than try to control them through reason. 'Morals excite passions, and produce or prevent actions' whereas 'reason is perfectly inert'.[19] Your 'moral sense' guides you towards behaviour that gives pleasure both to you and others. It's informed by feelings of sympathy and modified by our awareness of the conventions and rules of society. Although there are no objective moral facts, anarchy is prevented because, Hume thought, human nature is fundamentally benevolent.

Lesson 6: deep down, ethical behaviour is guided by how you *feel* about other people. You should act in ways that not only give you pleasure, but make other people happier too. This is what it means to have empathy.

Reason Above All

Despite Hume's modern view that emotions can act as internal barometers of what is right and pleasing, reason stayed in the ascendant, especially in the works of ultra-rationalist Immanuel Kant. He said while you have natural desires directed at your own good, rather than just following their promptings, you need to impose a moral law on yourself. This should be based on the principle that any action you are considering would be seen as right by everyone else, without contradiction. You should ask: 'what would everyone else do in the same circumstances?'[20] If you answer that everyone else would do exactly the same thing, then you can go ahead. This is a rational form of empathy.

Kant stressed the fact that you have autonomy, an ability to override emotions and appetites to develop rules of behaviour for yourself. This autonomy is a profound form of freedom. It gives you an entitlement not to be used instrumentally by others. He said: 'Act in such a way that you always treat humanity ... never simply as a means, but always at the same time as an end'.[21] As A.C. Grayling put it: 'Kant saw that free-willed beings are the most

---

19 David Hume, *A Treatise of Human Nature*, Book 3 (1738).
20 Kant called this way of thinking a 'categorical imperative': 'I ought never to act except in such a way that I can also will that my maxim should become a universal law'. Immanuel Kant, *Groundwork of the Metaphysic of Morals*, trans. H.J. Paton (Harper & Row, 1964), 70. See also George Chryssides and John H. Kaler, *An Introduction to Business Ethics* (Cengage Learning, 1993), 98.
21 Kant, *Groundwork*, 96.

valuable things in the world; they are "ends in themselves" which should never be treated instrumentally as means to other ends'.[22]

> **Lesson 7**: people are autonomous and profoundly free. That's why employees should never just be used as a means to an end, but treated as ends in themselves. The happiness and fulfillment of employees should be right at the top of the organisation's agenda for no other reason than that is the right thing to do.

The Pleasure Principle

Although Jeremy Bentham first published *An Introduction to the Principles of Morals and Legislation* in 1789, it wasn't widely read until its second edition in 1823. Bentham followed the Epicurean tradition, believing human nature is driven by the pleasure principle. His very first words are:

> *Nature has placed mankind under the governance of two sovereign masters, pain and pleasure. It is for them alone to point out what we ought to do, as well as to determine what we shall do.*

This principle, he felt, should be understood to operate not just at the individual level but for society as a whole. He saw it as providing a way for legislators to work out what rules to put in place by calculating whether, on balance, their laws created more pleasure than pain. He saw the 'felicific calculus' as an objective method of ensuring 'the greatest happiness of the greatest number that is the measure of right or wrong'. As Professor Alan Ryan[23] puts it:

> *His ultimate ambition was to construct a code of such simplicity that everyone might carry an abridgment of it in his pocket, and know his rights and duties as easily as he might nowadays look up the time of a train.*

There are many difficulties with this idea, which received the label of 'utilitarianism',[24] not least the danger of a majority enjoying pleasures at

---

22 A.C. Grayling, *What is Good?* (Phoenix, 2003), 151.
23 Alan Ryan (ed.), *John Stuart Mill and Jeremy Bentham* (Penguin Classics, 1993), 29.
24 The *Oxford Companion to Philosophy* says: 'Utilitarianism is an approach to morality that treats pleasure or desire-satisfaction as the sole element in human good and that regards the

the cost of a minority. Also, as J.S. Mill later pointed out, when it comes to measuring pleasures you can't just count them, you need to take their qualitative dimensions into account; some pleasures are much greater than others. But Bentham's heart was in the right place; unlike many of his contemporaries he did not believe the poor should suffer in silence. He wanted to find a way of moving towards a society where far more people could be happy. He wanted social progress.

> **Lesson 8**: looked at from the point of view of society, as well as that of the individual, a measured increase in happiness is the best guide to whether the world is improving or not. The underlying message for the twenty-first century is that material prosperity must be accompanied by an increase in happiness across the world in order to validate the workings of the global economy.

The Ethics of Progress

The nineteenth century brought the Big Idea of Evolution. Do ethics evolve? Both Herbert Spencer and Charles Darwin thought so.

Spencer went back to the days of early man and described how moral laws emerged so that communities could begin to make progress rather than tearing each other to pieces. His ethical first principle was the 'Law of Equal Freedom': 'Every man has the freedom to do all that he will, provided he infringes not the equal freedom of any other man'.[25] Like many other thinkers in the nineteenth century Spencer is an idealist. He believed 'the ultimate development of the ideal man is logically certain ... Progress, therefore, is not an accident but a necessity'.[26] But what kind of progress? To our eyes Spencer's ethics took an unfortunate turn when he suggested that no one, including the state, should interfere with the working of social 'adaptation' (his word for 'evolution'). Only the fittest should survive.

In his *Descent of Man* (1871) Darwin set out to provide an evolutionist account of the moral sense. He thought it was a type of instinct that worked in favour of survival. For Darwin, the whole point of morality was that it permitted 'the rearing of the greatest number of individuals in full vigour and health, with all the faculties perfect'. Looking ahead, he thought the evolution of morality

---

morality of actions as entirely dependent on consequences for human well being' (Oxford University Press, 2005), 936.

25 Herbert Spencer, *Social Statics* (The Online Library of Liberty, [1851]), Chapter 6, 1, 67.
26 Spencer, *Social Statics*, Chapter 2, 4, 44.

would continue as a natural process. He too was an idealist in thinking that man would eventually succeed in throwing off his aggressive instincts, that he was 'endeavouring to change that part of the moral sense which experience ... shows does not tend to [the] greatest good'.[27]

The ethics of progress took a different direction in the writing of Karl Marx. He saw ethical life as a social phenomenon. People are taught to obey the prevailing norms. The economic system, with its power structures, shapes the ethical norms in its own favour. For the oppressed classes this causes alienation and misery. He thought there would be an historic struggle resulting in the triumph of the masses over the few. At heart he was an idealist. He looked forward to people living a good life in which individual productive powers would be highly developed, and a working environment in which people would be able to express their creativity in an atmosphere of mutual respect and support. Marx's community, like Kant's, would be one where people are no longer used instrumentally but would be free to flourish. The appeal of this aspect of Marxist thinking would still be fresh today were it not for the fact it has been buried under tons of ideological rubble.

Lesson 9: ethical codes should not be set in stone. They must be adjusted and fine-tuned as society and its technologies continue to change. These changes should come from the people, from the aggregated wisdom of all. This can only be achieved through continuous dialogue.

Cry for Freedom

The first major work on ethics in the twentieth century appeared in 1903. In G.E. Moore's *Principia Ethica* he said that 'good' cannot be analysed. It's like the colour yellow; you can't describe it, you can only point to it. You can't break it down into constituent parts like 'beauty' or 'pleasure'. There is no link, he said, between goodness and happiness. Instead he argued that 'good states of mind' are the best form of the good, including 'affection for good and beautiful persons'. By focusing on states of mind, Moore was understood by the younger generation of this period to be freeing them up to think more widely about what is good, instead of slavishly following a Victorian moral code. This message had a liberating effect on the young John Maynard Keynes, who was

---

27 From Darwin, *Old and Useless Notes*, quoted in Darrin McMahon, *The Pursuit of Happiness* (Penguin, 2006), 413.

to transform economic thinking in the decades to come. Keynes's biographer, Robert Skidelsky, writes:

> [Keynes] tried to combine a personal ideal of civilised living with the championship of causes which would bring the good life – good states of mind – within the reach of the many. Management of the economy was the chief of these.[28]

A.J. Ayer's *Language, Truth and Logic* became something of a sensation after the Second World War. Stefan Collini[29] calls it 'one of the cultural reference points' of the decade. Like Moore's *Principia* it had a liberating effect on the post-war younger generation. They read that any statements that cannot be verified, like moral statements, are literally meaningless. In language, Ayer wrote, only statements that logically contain truth or falsity within the language itself (as in mathematics for example) or factual statements that can be proved or disproved by looking at the world (like scientific statements) have any meaning at all. By contrast, ethical statements are merely expressions of inner feelings, reflecting emotions. Modern logic denied any meaning whatsoever to religious statements.

Meanwhile, in a café somewhere in Paris, thinkers were discussing another way of looking at the good life that received the label 'existentialism'. Jean Paul Sartre argued that the ultimate human good is freedom, which entailed individuals facing up honestly to the sometimes absurd conditions of human existence and taking personal responsibility for all the choices they make. Despite the constraints we all work under, Sartre said that, in order to live an authentic life, we should be prepared to transform ourselves first and foremost by accepting that nothing determines our response to any situation – it's up to us what we do. We shouldn't blame others or circumstances for our actions. His utopia was filled with people who are both end and means for each other, where recognition of the 'other' is complete and where control is shared.

This call echoed across the Western world where, for many, there was no longer a God to provide ethical instructions. It had become a world in which people needed to create their own meanings. Sartre acknowledged that this was a hard and difficult path to follow, that a great deal of social change would be needed before his dreams would be fulfilled.

---

28 Robert Skidelsky, *John Maynard Keynes* (Pan Books, 2004), 289.
29 Stefan Collini, *Absent Minds: Intellectuals in Britain* (Oxford University Press, 2006), 393–409.

> **Lesson 10**: freedom from old conventions, freedom from tired language, freedom from our own conditioned ways of thinking – these appeals put the emphasis on individuals thinking for themselves. The message for the twenty-first century is clear – for creativity and innovation to flourish, orthodoxy needs to be constantly challenged. Progress depends on new ways of thinking, new states of mind.

Conversational Ethics

Another important strand of ethical thought emerged in the twentieth century, which had enquiry, discussion and debate at its core. Some of its most important exponents were American with all their experience of living in a society forged on principles of freedom, entrepreneurship and sheer dynamism. Let's look at two of them.

John Dewey saw all enquiry as practical problem solving. He saw that no moral rules or ethical principles are ever fixed or certain, but he was optimistic about social progress as he believed that intelligent individuals had the capacity to work things out through continuous enquiry. His great moral end-game was an increase in individuals' capacity for new experiences. Everything keeps changing, societies, institutions and new generations with new attitudes. Even individuals change their 'selves' as they grow older with different desires and ideals. This means that the search for what is good remains continuous and endless. Every generation must find its own answers by a continuous process of enquiry and discussion.

Towards the end of the twentieth century, another pragmatic thinker, Richard Rorty, went out of his way to describe philosophy, including ethics, as a conversational process. Rather than trying to work out what is 'real' or 'true', he said you should examine your beliefs and attitudes to see whether they will help you achieve what you've set out to achieve. He urged people to give up the goal of 'getting things right' and instead enlarge the repertoire of individual and cultural self-descriptions. This can be achieved through a continuous exchange of ideas between each other, both face to face, and through literature where you can use your imagination to sense what it's like to be a completely different person. In his view, this is a liberating experience, one that helps you to become happier, freer, more flexible. 'The maturation of our concepts, and the increasing richness of our conceptual repertoire, constitute cultural progress'.[30]

---

30 Richard Rorty, *The Rorty Reader* (Wiley-Blackwell, 2010), 195–203.

Rather than worrying about essences, we should concentrate on 'how we can arrange things so as to be comfortable with one another, how institutions can be changed so that everyone's right to be understood has a better chance of being gratified'.[31]

Lesson 11: pragmatism, as a way of approaching problem solving, is ideally suited to organisations dealing with rapid change. The pragmatic way forward for ethics in the workplace is to build ethics into a continuous conversation. Ethics at work should match the changing wants and desires of employees who need to be trusted to find the right answers.

Human Rights at Work

If ethics are a set of agreements about how to behave towards each other that change over time, fundamental human rights are timeless and universal. Is it odd to talk about human rights in the context of organisational life? Not at all. Power structures of command and control can often inflict severe constraints on individuals. As James Hoopes says:

> we ignore the fact that we check many of our freedoms at the workplace door and that ordinary citizens get their closest exposure to undemocratic government when they go to work for a corporation.[32]

Since the Second World War there has been a huge increase in activity aimed at protecting human rights around the world. An enormous amount of work has been put into defining universal rights.[33] When you look at the five so-called 'first generation rights', you will see they apply to employees as much as to anyone else. They are:

1.   Freedom of inquiry and expression.
2.   Due process of law/fair procedures.
3.   Equal treatment free of discrimination or bias.
4.   Freedom from cruel treatment – physical or mental.
5.   Right to privacy – no intrusion into private space.

---

31 Rorty, *The Rorty Reader*, 307–20.
32 James Hoopes, *False Prophets* (Perseus Publishing, 2003), xiv.
33 See Aryeh Neier, *The International Human Rights Movement: A History* (Princeton University Press, 2012).

These rights should apply to employees in Beijing and Tokyo as much as London and New York – they are universal rights. It's immediately obvious, though, how command and control structures can have a negative impact on all of them.

In many organisations employees are not free to ask for certain types of information and are unable to express their views. In the more advanced organisations throughout the world a lot of work has gone into improving procedures and reducing discrimination, but unfair and prejudiced managers still exist everywhere. Physical and mental harms are still experienced by many employees. It's increasingly difficult for many to switch off from work to enjoy private time.

Lesson 12: PROGRESSIVE ORGANISATIONS will establish simple and clear ethical guidelines that protect human rights. They will follow the spirit of Article 1 of the UN's Universal Declaration of Human Rights,[34] which reads: 'All human beings [i.e. employees] are born free and equal in dignity and rights. They are endowed with reason and conscience and should act towards one another in a spirit of brotherhood.' They will agree with the premise that unethical behaviour reduces trust between organisations, their employees, suppliers, customers and the countries they operate in. This, in turn, reduces their efficiency and the extent to which they can contribute to social progress.

The 12 Lessons Summarised

From this short tour of ideas about ethics, 12 lessons have been distilled. They're summarised below, with particular reference to organisations. These lessons provide a framework within which Principled Persuasion can operate to best effect. You can decide whether you agree with them or not.

1. Widespread agreement on ethical norms helps stop the 'mighty' from dominating everyone else.
2. It's best to formulate ethical codes by means of reasonable questions, discussions and persuasive arguments.
3. Taking control over yourself, and accepting personal responsibility, is the only way ethical codes can work in practice.
4. Religious beliefs should be respected but treated with caution.
5. Listening to your inner self, then agreeing principles with others, is how understanding on ethics is reached.

---

34 For the full text go to www.un.org/en/documents/udhr/index.shtml

6.   You should be sensitive to your emotions and follow those feelings that give you, and others, pleasure.

7.   Your happiness at work, and that of others, is an end in itself.

8.   The extent to which your organisation is increasing the happiness of employees is a key indicator of progress and future success.

9.   Ethics evolve, so the organisational discussion on ethics needs to be continuous.

10.   Ethics, in the PROGRESSIVE ORGANISATION, will encourage free individuals to challenge orthodoxy.

11.   A pragmatic approach to ethics in organisations entails tuning into the needs and wants of employees.

12.   High visibility ethics are vital to the protection of fundamental human rights at work.

The Principles of Ethical Persuasion

If you do agree with these 12 lessons, you will probably also feel the need for a further distillation of these concepts so that they can be more easily embedded in communication strategy. So here it is. Looking across the landscape of ethical theories, it's possible to see four outstanding features:

- the importance of mankind's unique gift of reason;
- the role of pleasure and pain in guiding behaviour;
- the need for empathy to make communities work;
- the concept of individual human dignity.

These four features can be turned into Principles of Ethical Persuasion that can be used to guide the process of integrating ethics into all forms of organisational communication. Research and feedback mechanisms should identify the specific ethical practices to be highlighted and discussed in each organisation.

Principle 1: Encourage reflection on ethical principles

The PROGRESSIVE ORGANISATION will prompt people to ask questions about what's right and wrong, and deliberate on the ethical matters that are important to their working lives. They must feel able to challenge established practices that they see as unethical. Principled Persuaders will provide a continuous stream of material to inform those debates, including examples of ethical dilemmas. This principle taps into employees' ability to use their unique gift of reason to work through the ethical uncertainties of everyday life at work. It will help them develop their moral sense.

Principle 2: Use the Happiness and Harm Profiles to construct ethical norms

There's no escaping the fundamental importance of maximising pleasure and minimising pain. It comes up over and over again in theories about ethics. It's just that the concept can't survive by itself. Too many people get pleasure from harming others. That's why Principled Persuaders should use the information they have about what actually goes on within the organisation to put forward ethical norms for employees to agree.

Principle 3: Promote the advantages of diversity

Empathy for others lies at the heart of ethical behaviour. This involves shedding prejudice and being open minded to very different points of view. Principled Persuaders should use communication to help employees 'put themselves in other people's shoes'. Communities made up from diverse beliefs, held together by agreement on what constitutes ethical behaviour towards each other, are more likely to be interesting, creative and fun.

Principle 4: Emphasise the importance of everyone being treated with dignity

Employees should not be seen solely as a means to an end. The happiness of employees is an end in itself. Because organisations are goal-oriented, the temptation is to treat employees as raw material or 'human resources'. A change of mindset is needed here on the part of many senior managers. Only by treating all employees with dignity, which includes accepting their entitlement to freedom of expression, will leaders be able to supplement their power with moral authority.

Psychologists tell us there are a number of stages in the development of moral sense in the individual. First along are instincts modified by reward and punishment (pleasure/pain – praise/blame). Experience of rewards and punishments gradually conditions young people to conform to ethical norms. As they mature, they accept the necessity for constraints on freedom, such as laws, to keep social order. At the final stage comes justification of ethical codes through a belief in universal principles. At this point you might say they have a good level of 'moral intelligence'.

Like IQ, moral intelligence is unevenly distributed amongst the population. That's why the Principles of Ethical Persuasion are designed to help individual employees grow in awareness and understanding of the need for ethical behaviour that respects differences. One researcher[35] has described the characteristics of the individuals who achieve high levels of moral intelligence as follows:

> The people who develop in moral judgment are those who love to learn, who seek new challenges, who enjoy intellectually stimulating environments, who are reflective, who make plans and set goals, who take risks, who see themselves in the larger social contexts of history and institutions and broad cultural trends, who take responsibility for themselves and their environs.

It may be asking too much of Principled Persuasion to convert every employee into such a paragon, but it's the right direction to take.

---

35 James R. Rest, *Moral Development* (Praeger, 1986), quoted in Steven Bartlett, *The Pathology of Man: A Study of Human Evil* (Charles C. Thomas, 2005), 275.

PART III
MAKING CONVERSATION ALONG THE WAY

CHAPTER 7

Watch Your Language: The Principles of Meaningful Persuasion

If a lion could talk, we could not understand him.[1]

In ENGINEERED ORGANISATIONS, language is used to motivate and control. In PROGRESSIVE ORGANISATIONS, there is a conscious focus on language as the means to a rich, nourishing culture in which innovation and creativity can thrive. The creative role of language is to open up minds, introduce new thoughts and stimulate new conversations. A better use of language is the way to reduce communication friction – the thousands of misunderstandings and misperceptions that prevent the organisation from performing as well as it might.

Yet, in the average organisation, how many people have been trained to use language well? Not very many. It's taken for granted despite the fact that using language well requires skill. Just look at how many complaints there are in most organisations about 'poor communication'. This is not just a matter of channels; it's about the language that's used within the organisation. Principled Persuaders are sensitive to this issue. They know that it is easy for a great deal of communication to be wasted because of a poor use of language. So they are keen to promote a higher level of awareness amongst all employees of the need for clear, simple, expressive language.

How can you make the language you use more meaningful and effective? How can you be more certain that the messages you intend to send are

---

1   Ludwig Wittgenstein (1889–1951), who will be quoted a great deal in this chapter, was the leading analytical philosopher of the twentieth century. Born, in Vienna, into one of the richest families in Europe, he gave all his money away in order to concentrate on philosophy. He worked at Cambridge from 1929 until his death. His first masterpiece, *Tractatus Logico-Philosophicus*, was published in 1921, his second, *Philosophical Investigations*, two years after his death, in 1953. A completely original thinker, his views have inspired a great deal of new thought in the philosophies of language, psychology and mathematics.

accurately received? How can you avoid producing low impact communication that's weak and colourless?

To answer these questions, let's take a step backwards and have a good hard look at the nature of language. Where did it come from? What is it for? You'll see that, as a species, our use of a sophisticated verbal language is relatively recent. You'll note that humanity could not have crawled out of its caves without a growing vocabulary. You'll reflect on how slippery the meaning of words can be. You'll be amazed at the sudden rise of English to its status as a global language. And by the end of the chapter, you'll almost certainly agree that organisations need to put far more thought and analysis into the language they're using, and make greater provision for training people at all levels to communicate more clearly and effectively.

How Did Language Evolve?

Nobody knows for sure how language evolved but there are lots of educated guesses. The expert consensus is that when our early ancestors, the hominids, split away from bonobos and chimpanzees about six million years ago, their language would have been similar to that of our ape cousins. Over time, as hominids began to walk on two feet, the arms were freed up for a much wider range of gestures. Early language was most probably a combination of facial expressions, lip-smacks, teeth chattering and a variety of noises.

Fast forward four million years to about two million years ago and hominid brains begin to grow. As brain size increased enough language emerged to support more skilful tool making. But the real surge in human creativity took place around 40,000 years ago. They produced more sophisticated tools and began experimenting with body ornamentation and other art forms. It's probably around that time, or just before, that the larynx completed its move downwards into the throat. This opened up a space allowing the tongue[2] to move around. It created more vocal cavities for producing a wider range of sounds. As the nasal cavity could now be shut, the precision of sounds was greatly increased. Humans, uniquely in the animal kingdom, were now able to voice a multiplicity of resonances, pitches, accents and intonations.

Just making lots of different sounds is obviously not enough to constitute a language. The sounds needed to be organised into longer strings of words. This was the beginning of syntax, the rules by which you combine words in order to

---

2   The word 'language' derives from the Latin 'lingua' meaning 'tongue'.

make them into meaningful phrases. But how and when did all this take place? Was there a 'a soup of random and semi-random events'[3] out of which syntax gradually appeared? Or did the brain suddenly acquire a facility for language as Noam Chomsky suggested? From the late 1950s to the 1990s Noam Chomsky put forward theories about language development that remain controversial. He said every human child seems to know instinctively how to acquire words and grammar, quite rapidly. He argued the brain must contain something like a software programme, probably consisting of different modules, that allows children to throw the appropriate mental switches and begin speaking in the language of their parents.

What is certain is that language became the chief engine of human progress, allowing our species to dominate all others. Language is universal in all human beings. No tribe has ever been discovered without a language.[4] It comes naturally to us all.

Acquiring Language

There is a direct relationship between the richness of your thought and the development of your language skills. The more words you have at your disposal, the more productive your thought processes can be. Psychologists, studying the development of language in children, have provided evidence of a universal ability to learn quickly. Babies start to babble at about 7–8 months. The sounds they make are much the same in all cultures. By 12 months they're voicing simple words; at 18 months they're practising grammar. The rate of acquisition of vocabulary is outstanding. It's estimated[5] that a two-year-old actively uses 500 words, a three-year-old 1,000, a five-year-old up to 3,000. By the age of six the average child can recognise (though not use) up to 14,000 words. From babyhood through to late adolescence children learn ten new words every day. This takes them to 20,000 words by 13 and, depending on level of education, to over 50,000 by 20 years of age. As with vocabulary so with grammar. According to Stephen Pinker, at the age of three years there is an 'explosion' of grammatical

---

3   Alison Wray, *The Transition to Language* (Oxford University Press, 2002), 1.
4   When explorers began to meet the isolated tribes of the New Guinea highlands in the 1930s, they discovered that, in a population of around one million people, there were 800 languages.
5   Steven Pinker, *The Language Instinct* (The Folio Society, 2008 [1994]), 226–9; Jean Aitchison, *Words in the Mind* (Blackwell Publishing, 1987), 188.

usage with 90 per cent accuracy. It's the few mistakes that are so noticeable and cute.

Your language makes you what you are. It not only projects your identity to others, it provides you with a tool-kit for thinking. Wittgenstein said: 'The limits of my language mean the limits of my world'.[6] Hominids of around 700,000 years ago had a level of language roughly equivalent to that of a two-year-old child today. They couldn't achieve much with such a limited amount of language. Your vocabulary is a good indicator of the size of your mental world. An academic in a specialist field, with a vocabulary of, say, 100,000 words, is going to be able to encompass more thoughts and concepts than a student ticking over on 50,000.

In a typical day you use about 8,000 words, a fraction of the total available to you. Nevertheless, that's plenty to help you negotiate your way through the day, doing ordinary things. You'll also probably dip into the vocabularies of working life and your interests like sport or the arts. It seems pretty easy to make yourself understood. It's not often that you struggle to find the right word. Yet, the funny thing about communication is its ability to trip you up when you least expect it. Because it's acquired so naturally, because you don't give a huge amount of thought to the words you use except in special situations, it's easy to be misunderstood. What's more, you often don't realise that you have been misunderstood, that someone is taking out a completely different meaning from the one you intended. Meaning is a slippery beast.

What Do You Mean?

Language can be used in ways that conceals more than it reveals. Assumptions are made that people are fully receiving the intended message. This is expecially true in organisations where a lot of communication can turn into meaningless 'non-sense', especially when management-speak is at its worst. In fact, communication from managers often uses words that have quite different meanings for employees. For example, managers say 'more flexibility', employees take out 'more uncertainty'; 'portfolio career' = 'insecurity'; 'empowerment' = 'more work for same money'; 'engagement' = 'work harder for love of the organisation'; 'people assets' = 'slaves'. OK, maybe the last one goes a bit far, but you get the point.

---

6   Ludwig Wittgenstein, *Tractatus Logico-Philosophicus*, trans. D.F. Pears and B.F. McGuiness (Routledge, 1997 [1921]), 56.

That the same word carrying different meanings causes confusion is illustrated by this example. A philosopher called Heraclitus posed the question 'Can you step into the same river twice?' His answer was that you couldn't, provoking centuries of philosophical argument. Then Wittgenstein pointed out the dilemma was resolved once you defined what you meant by 'river'. Clearly, each time you stepped into the river the water had changed. So does river mean the water itself or a channel along which water is flowing? Most people would opt for the latter and therefore answer yes to the original question. It's the same river, just different water.

Try this thought experiment on the meaning of words. It's called 'Wittgenstein's beetle'.

> *Suppose everyone had a box with something in it: we call it a 'beetle'. No one can look into anyone else's box, and everyone says that he knows what a beetle is only by looking at his beetle. Here it would be quite possible for everyone to have something different in his box. One might even imagine such a thing constantly changing. But suppose the word 'beetle' had a use in these people's language? If so it would not be used as the name of a thing. The thing in the box has no place in the language-game at all; not even as a something: for the box might even be empty.[7]*

You can be using a particular word with somebody, but you're both talking about different things. As you can't see into someone else's head (the box) you'll never know – unless you agree on a definition beforehand, which is rare. Now, in everyday speech, this might not matter so much. Meanings can be approximate. It's just not practical to define meanings in every conversation – it would never get finished. If you say 'I'm tired – let's go home' it would be strange for the other person to ask 'What exactly do you mean by tired?' You could be exhausted or just slightly fatigued; you could be mentally drained or physically weary or both. It hardly matters – the meaning is enough to get agreement to go home.

But in organisations it is important to be precise about what words mean, especially words that are repeated over and over again. They should be defined, and those definitions should be easily accessible to everyone. Efforts should be made to test what employees understand these key words to mean. The very process of asking senior managers to give some thought to the meaning of

---

7   Ludwig Wittgenstein, *Philosophical Investigations*, trans. G.E.M. Anscombe (Blackwell, 2001 [1953]), 100.

the words they habitually use, would almost certainly throw up differences of opinion between them.

In 1939, a speech by the politician Herbert Morrison was found to have contained more than 50 words not understood by his audience, including 'issues', 'evolution' and 'fundamental'.[8] Employees are more educated than that these days, but it's a fair bet that a good number of words used by senior managers and others in organisations have little or no meaning for many employees. After all, 29 per cent of the British workforce are currently below level 2 in education (that's A–C grades in GCSEs) and have just around 10,000 naming words in their vocabulary on average.[9]

Writing and Speech

Within the great time-span of humanity's development, writing in its crudest form appeared only yesterday, about 5,000 years ago. The Greek alphabet emerged around 800 BC. Whoever invented it was a genius. Instead of using pictures to carry meanings, someone thought of using symbols that allow us to reproduce the sounds of speech. The Romans modified the Greek letters to form the basis of the script you're reading now.

Writing is a large step removed from speech. It's much easier to make your meaning clear through speech than through writing. In his dialogue with Phaedrus,[10] Socrates says:

> there's something odd about writing, Phaedrus, which makes it exactly like painting. The offspring of painting stand there as if alive, but if you ask them a question they maintain an aloof silence. It's the same with written words: you might think they were speaking as if they had some intelligence, but if you want an explanation of any of the things they are saying and you ask them about it, they just go on and on for ever giving the same single piece of information.

Words on a page can't be interrogated. You can't ask them 'what do you mean?' and receive an explanation as you can in a conversation. This makes it all the more important that writers are not only careful in their use of words, making

---

8   Jonathan Rose, *The Intellectual Life of the British Working Classes* (Yale Nota Bene, 2002), 223.

9   See the National Literacy Trust at literacytrust.org.uk for more information.

10 Plato, *Phaedrus*, trans. Robin Waterfield (Oxford World Classic Edition, 2009), 70.

sure that unusual words are properly explained, they should also provide the right amount of context so the reader is able to understand fully what is meant. Context might consist of historical background, definition of words, explanation of concepts and so on.

That's why Principled Persuaders need to 'stand back' and evaluate the possible meanings of text from the point of view of someone who doesn't have the same background knowledge. They understand that authors are subject to their own limitations of thought and conditioned by sometimes unconscious beliefs that emerge in the text. From this perspective, language is never a wholly transparent and neutral conveyer of thought. Use of language often reflects hidden prejudices and biases. Critical analysis of texts within organisations helps identify those areas of communication that need to be made more meaningful.

Speech provides far more clues to meaning than written texts. Gestures, facial expressions, the volume, intensity and pitch of speech communicate emotions and send signals to the hearer that put the words into a particular context. Even a simple sound like 'Ah' can be pronounced in a tone of surprise, disappointment, resignation or grumpiness and convey quite different meanings. Yet few people have been trained to use face-to-face speech effectively. One of the biggest problems of communication within organisations is the lack of awareness people have about their own speech patterns and habits. How many, for example, know that speech breaks down into nine basic modes?[11]

In modern organisations speech is a form of action. The vast majority of communication is carried out face-to-face. Many mistakes in communication are made through lack of awareness of the way speech works. The nine modes of speech are: inquiry, probing, diagnosis, articulation, advocacy, advice, critiquing, challenge and admonishment. If any of these modes is used excessively or inappropriately, the wrong messages are likely to be sent. Conversations are all too often counterproductive because of a lack of mindfulness as to the appropriate mode of speech to employ. The PROGRESSIVE ORGANISATION will put interpersonal speech training at the top of its communication agenda.

The Need for Clarity

Muddle-minded communication is hardly new. In 1561 Thomas Hobbes wrote:

---

11   This draws on the concept of VoicePrint, owned by Business Cognition Ltd. For more information see www.ocl-voiceprint.com

> *a man that seeketh precise truth, had need to remember what every*
> *name he uses stands for; and to place it accordingly; or else he will*
> *find himself entangled in words, as a bird in lime twigs; the more he*
> *struggles, the more belimed.*[12]

He was especially critical of the scholastics, the academics of the time, for using 'insignificant trains of strange and barbarous words' that 'hath a quality, not only to hide the truth, but also to make men think they have it, and desist from further search'.[13] Does that remind you of management-speak? Just over one hundred years later, John Locke agreed:

> *The chief end of language in communication being to be understood,*
> *words serve not well for that end ... when any word does not excite in*
> *the hearer the same idea which it stands for in the mind of the speaker.*[14]

Three hundred years after that comment Ludwig Wittgenstein pointed out that it is quite possible to produce perfectly comprehensible phrases that have nothing corresponding to them in the real world, such as 'a golden mountain'. Several decades later, in the 1960s, Noam Chomsky used this short sentence, 'Colourless green ideas sleep furiously', to illustrate how a recognisably grammatical phrase can be totally devoid of sense. Language can beguile us into meaninglessness.

There is much greater awareness nowadays of the need to eliminate clichés and jargon in the text churned out by organisations. Movements such as the Plain English Campaign[15] have worked hard to promote the meaningful use of English. George Orwell would have been pleased with their efforts. This distinguished writer had strong views on the way language was used by politicians and other professionals. In his 'Essay on the English People' written in May 1944 he said:

> *Whoever writes English is involved in a struggle that never lets up*
> *even for a sentence. He is struggling against vagueness, against*
> *obscurity, against the lure of the decorative adjective, against the*

---

12 Thomas Hobbes, *Leviathan* (Oxford World Classics, 1998 [1651]), Part 1, Chapter 4, 12, 23.
13 Hobbes, *Leviathan*, Part 4, Chapter 46, 40, 455.
14 John Locke, *An Essay Concerning Human Understanding* (Ward, Lock & Co., 1900 [1689]), Book 2, Chapter 20, 2, 160.
15 For many examples of jargon and incomprehensible text see: www.plainenglish.co.uk

encroachment of Latin and Greek, and, above all, against the worn out
phrases and dead metaphors with which the language is cluttered up.

In his essay 'Politics and the English Language' (April 1946) he attacks political language as giving 'an appearance of solidity to pure wind'. The same criticisms could be applied to a great deal of communication material produced by organisations today. Orwell set out some guidelines for a better use of English, as follows:

1. Never use a metaphor, simile, or other figure of speech which you are used to seeing in print.
2. Never use a long word where a short one will do.
3. If it is possible to cut a word out, always cut it out.
4. Never use the passive where you can use the active.
5. Never use a foreign phrase, a scientific word, or a jargon word if you can think of an everyday English equivalent.
6. Break any of these rules sooner than say anything outright barbarous.

Not everybody can stick to all of these rules all of the time, especially under the pressure of deadlines. Principled Persuaders will do all they can to eliminate clichés and jargon from their communications. Yet, within many organisations at the moment it is possible to find examples of bland, boring text at best, and meaningless gibberish at worst. Why is this?

One explanation is that it's much easier to default to the well-worn phrase, the cliché that's hard to argue with, the expressions that will meet with approval from senior managers because they don't say very much. In 1940, Eric Partridge produced his *Dictionary of Clichés*.[16] When you read through it you realise just how hard they are to avoid.

Here are just a few of the examples he gave then that are still going strong now: 'the burning question'; 'deliver the goods'; 'go the extra mile'; 'grasp the nettle'; 'second to none'; 'in a nutshell'; 'a striking example'. A modern example of cliché-ridden management-speak might be:

Going forward, we need some blue-sky thinking that really pushes
the envelope. Let's take it to the next level and move the goal posts on
this mission critical set of issues.

---

16 The word cliché is from the French verb meaning 'to stereotype' and was used in the die-sinking trade, the process of engraving patterns for printing on objects like coins.

In day to day speech there is probably nothing wrong with using clichés – they move things along when we're not too bothered about the effect of our words. But it does matter in communication that's meant to be persuasive and inspiring. Clichés can be seen as so thin in meaning that all they're doing is taking up space. Wittgenstein said: 'A wheel that can be turned though nothing else moves with it, is not part of the mechanism'.[17] A perfect description of clichés and meaningless words.

Jargon is different. It's not meaningless to most of its practitioners, though it is possible to question someone spouting jargon only to find they have no idea what the words they're using actually mean. Chaucer used the word 'jargon' to refer to the twittering of birds. Later it came to mean the 'anti-language' used by thieves and other criminals to communicate without alerting people to what they were doing.[18] By the seventeenth century 'cant' and 'jargon' were interchangeable words and referred to the language used by professionals such as doctors and lawyers. There was more and more of it around, and in the eighteenth century Dr Johnson advised: 'Clear your mind of cant'.

Jargon in the professions served a number of purposes: it acted as a verbal shorthand for faster communication; using it showed you were a member of a privileged group; it served as a barrier to outsiders, protecting the status (and income) of the professional classes; in the case of people like quack doctors it concealed their ignorance, making them sound far more learned than they were. Jargon is used to exclude as much as to include. If you're not sure of the meaning of jargon words, it shows you're not in the swim. Accordingly a great deal of nonsense in organisations goes unchallenged as employees are loath to reveal what looks like their own ignorance.

It is harder to argue against the use of jargon as a form of shorthand, enabling a swift exchange of technical meanings in a specialist field. But there is every reason to argue with jargon that spreads itself outside this boundary and, like a virus, takes over the healthy body of plain English. In the twenty-first century it remains all-pervasive, even in books on the use of language. Take this example from an academic book on how to communicate: 'We hit on the same referent by appealing to solvability, sufficiency and joint salience'. Maybe academics can

---

17   Wittgenstein, *Philosophical Investigations*, 95.

18   This function of jargon was still going strong in the twentieth century. In the 1930s to early 1970s Polari was a language used by the gay community. Here's an example followed by its 'translation': 'Ooh vada well the omee-palone ajax who just trolled in – she's got nanti taste, dear, cod lolly-drags and the naff riah but what a bona eek. Fantabulosa' ('Have a good look at that homo who just came in. He's got no taste – awful trousers and tasteless hair – but what a lovely face. Absolutely fabulous'). Diego Gambetta, *Codes of the Underworld* (Princeton University Press, 2009), 156.

be excused as they are often writing for fellow academics, but it's questionable whether even specialists can understand this dense jargon.

English: A Young, Still Growing Language

Languages are born, grow to maturity and die, just like living creatures. Some of them give birth to other languages. Linguists say 10,000 years is the maximum life span of a language before all traces of it have disappeared in its descendants. Many languages have come and gone already. At the present time there are around 6,000 languages on the planet, of which only 600 are relatively secure due to the number of speakers. That means as many as 90 per cent of these languages could be extinct by the turn of the twenty-second century. By then, English is likely to be more dominant than ever.

Never, in the history of the world, has one language been spoken by so many people. Around two billion[19] people can now communicate in some form of English. That's way ahead of the next most spoken language, Mandarin, at 1.3 billion. Yet English as we know it has only been evolving for around 1,500 years, a mere teenager in language terms. How is it that such a young language has sprung up into such a prominent position throughout much of the world?

The story of English takes us from a motley collection of barbarian tribes in one small part of the planet right through to today's international, globalised community of English speakers. In the fifth century AD, the total population of Britain was around half a million people, highly fragmented into lots of little tribes. Britons, Scots, Picts and Celts, amongst others, spoke their own languages. Some Latin speakers were still around, a legacy of the Roman conquest.

Then in 449 AD the first Germans arrived, by boat, near Ramsgate. Britain became even more multi-ethnic and multi-lingual. Over time the mysterious alchemy of language began to fuse dialects together. One in particular, West Saxon, became a standard literary dialect we know as 'Old English' under the sponsorship of King Alfred (849–899 AD). He made it his mission to promote Christianity by making West Saxon a language common[20] to different tribes. The strong Germanic influence on English was to last another two to three

---

19 Mikael Parkvall, *Limits of Language* (Battlebridge Publications, 2006), 57.
20 It's worth noting that the word 'communicate' comes from the Latin 'communico' which not only means 'to inform', but also 'to share' and 'to unite'. The idea of 'community' is intrinsic to 'communication'.

centuries but by the early Middle Ages it had begun to wane. New ways of ordering words produced a new language called 'Middle English'.

Following the Norman Conquest of 1066 AD, Britain remained a thick stew of different dialects. The upper classes were trilingual. Latin was the unchallenged language of the church and scholarship. French was the language of the court and officialdom. But neither Latin nor French was able to gain ground amongst ordinary people. Whilst Latin remained an important language in Britain amongst the educated classes right up to the twentieth century, French dropped out. It became the language of the enemy when English descendants of William the Conqueror fell out with their French cousins in the fourteenth century.

Meanwhile English continued to evolve rapidly to the point where it was becoming recognisable as the ancestor of modern English. The amazing change that had taken place in the language can be illustrated by comparing the Old English in the poem *Beowulf* (tenth century) with lines from Chaucer's *Canterbury Tales* (fourteenth century).

Here are the opening lines from Beowulf followed by Seamus Heaney's translation:[21]

> *Hwæt! We Gardena in geardagum,*
> *þeodcyninga, þrym gefrunon,*
> *hu ða æþelingas ellen fremedon.*
> *So. The Spear-Danes in days gone by*
> *and the kings who ruled them had courage and greatness.*
> *We have heard of those princes' heroic campaign.*

Now the opening lines of Chaucer's 'Knight's Tale':

> *Whilom, as olde stories tellen us,*
> *Ther was a duc that highte Theseus;*
> *Of Atthenes he was lord and governour.*

The Old English text is unreadable to modern eyes but, if you know 'highte' means 'called', the Chaucer is easily understood despite the spelling.

New words poured into the English vocabulary from Latin, French and other languages. It's estimated that 50,000 words in modern English come directly from Latin, and 30,000 from French. The English vocabulary increased

---

21   Seamus Heaney, *Beowulf* (Faber & Faber, 1999), 2.

from about 50,000 words in 1100 AD to around 150,000 by 1600. More words gave more options. For example, by 1500 AD it was possible to 'ask' (Old English), to 'question' (French) and to 'interrogate' (Latin). From the sixteenth to the eighteenth centuries English vocabulary grew and grew. Some words didn't survive but many did. New words were needed for the ideas flowing in from religion, science, and the discoveries of explorers. People were making up new words all the time. Scholars have identified over 1,700 words invented by Shakespeare alone.

'Anarchy' first appeared as an English word in 1539. By the eighteenth century it was being used to describe the state of the English language. Grammarians began exerting their influence. The first book of grammar appeared in 1586[22] but it was in 1750–1800 that the number of rules and regulations on the correct use of English began to multiply. Lindley Murray produced an English grammar in 1795 that sold 20 million copies, leaving a lasting imprint on the teaching of grammar in Britain well into the 1960s. In the late eighteenth century Dr Johnson published his dictionary, the fourth edition of which contained 43,729 entries, an impressive achievement but still only a fraction of the total vocabulary which, by then, was into the hundreds of thousands and still growing. In the nineteenth and twentieth centuries the continued influx of new words has taken modern English vocabulary to well over a million words.

English in the twenty-first century is the product of many nations. As many as 350 languages have directly contributed words to English vocabulary. The United States evolved its own version of English. In 1806, Noah Webster introduced a new standard of American English. His dictionary of 70,000 words, half of which were different from those in Dr Johnson's, contained simplified spellings, more in line with the way words sounded. Over time, as British colonies grew into an empire, forms of English were being widely spoken in India, Australia, West and South Africa, Canada and parts of South East Asia. Hybrid forms, like Creole, appeared in the Caribbean and Southern American states.

English, a vigorous adolescent in language terms, is still growing. It's not much of a prediction to say that billions more are likely to speak English later in the twenty-first century. Its use on the Internet, the ease of modern travel, the global need for a common language are all likely to underpin its rapid spread across the world. Many non-English-speaking peoples see learning English as

22 William Bullokar, *Pamphlet for Grammar* (1586).

opening a linguistic gateway to personal prosperity. What's more, they can join in the worldwide conversation that has really only just begun.

A World of Words

The philosopher John Locke believed that words were 'signs of ideas' that enabled 'the thoughts of men's minds [to] be conveyed from one to another'.[23] You can now see that it's not as easy as that. There are many barriers in the way of clear communication. Thomas Hobbes had a better idea when he wrote:

> men give different names to one and the same thing, from the differences of their own passions; as they that approve a private opinion, call it opinion – but they that mislike it, heresy.[24]

In modern terms, one person's freedom fighter is another's rebel or terrorist. Yet, it's precisely this capacity for interpreting the world's events in completely different ways that has given humanity the ability to make such awe-inspiring progress.

Diversity of opinion, and the debate that ensues, spurs the world forward. Just imagine the opposite. If everyone saw everything the same way, the human race would stultify, grind to a halt. That's why organisations need to be so much better at using language clearly and meaningfully. The poor use of language is holding organisations back. The lack of skills training in the use of language is astonishing given its importance in every aspect of an organisation's work.

Language conditions people and organisations. Words are not passive objects. They act in the world to shape people and events. People fight and die for concepts embodied in words like liberty or jihad. The American philosopher, Richard Rorty, focused on the power of words to achieve fundamental change. He pointed to the way you acquire your own personal vocabulary and ways of speaking. You're influenced by upbringing, family, friends, school, the workplace, your leisure and cultural activities. Each one of these influences contributes a set of vocabulary and verbal expressions. This verbal tool-kit makes you what you are.

But Rorty taught that you have the power to 'redescribe yourself' if you want to. You don't have to be stuck with the language you use. If you feel the

---

23 Locke, *Essay*, Book 3, Chapter 1, 2, 321.
24 Hobbes, *Leviathan*, Part 1, Chapter 2, 19, 69.

need to change direction in your life, or acquire a different identity, you can use words to redescribe yourself, to 'reweave the fabric of your beliefs and desires'.[25] A conscious effort to think in different ways about yourself, hard though it is, can lead to a major transformation in lifestyle.

So it is for organisations. A conscious effort to use language differently, to employ a vocabulary conducive to a happy, creative working environment, is a hallmark of the PROGRESSIVE ORGANISATION. Just as a painter chooses a pallette of colours, Principled Persuaders will make a careful choice of words to spur the organisation in a progressive direction. On the other hand, the ENGINEERED ORGANISATION is unlikely to give careful thought to its vocabulary. It will remain mired in the slushy terminology of Motivational Communication. The 'richness of its conceptual repertoire'[26] will be more limited than that of the PROGRESSIVE ORGANISATION.

The Principles of Meaningful Persuasion

The richness of an organisation's use of language is directly related to its capacity for creativity and innovation. The role of Principled Persuaders is to foster a rich, fertile climate of communication within which individual employees, and their ideas, can flourish. They know the pathway to a successful future in the twenty-first century lies through interesting and productive conversations at all levels in the organisation. Such conversations will be stimulated by meaningful persuasion based on these principles:

Principle 1: Develop an understanding of the organisation's key words

Using the latest methods of text analysis[27] identify the words and phrases most used in cascade communications, feedback channels and emails. Use research to check the received meanings of these words in a statistically valid cross-section of employees. Look for 'attitude gaps' between management and employees and other differences in interpretation. Plug the gaps with definitions.

---

25 Richard Rorty, *The Rorty Reader* (Wiley-Blackwell, 2010), 211–26.
26 Rorty, *The Rorty Reader*, 195–203.
27 This discipline has acquired a name of its own – 'culturomics'. Buzz-phrases associated with it are 'quantitative analysis of digitised text', 'text mining', 'sentiment scoring', 'emotion detecting'.

Principle 2: Introduce new words into the stream of communication

To encourage the development of an enriched and progressive culture, the vocabulary of happiness, mindfulness and ethics should be woven into all organisational discourse. This entails creating content in communication programmes that introduces and defines words that you want to become part of everyday language.

Principle 3: Improve everyone's speaking skills

This requires special effort. There's a lot of catching up to do as organisations have badly neglected this type of training. Employees at all levels need to be taught how to use different modes of voice to suit different contexts and occasions. Self-aware and skilled use of different voices by individuals will enormously enhance the productive value of face-to-face communication.

Principle 4: Minimise the use of clichés and jargon

Scour the organisation's written materials including all digital text for examples of poor English. Use the guides and software packages from organisations like the Plain English Campaign to track poor usage and educate employees in the importance of clear, meaningful text.

For many organisations even thinking about their use of language in this amount of detail will come as a new idea. Yet better communication is one of the great untapped sources of productivity improvement in all organisations. A clearer, more meaningful use of language, together with a rich and stimulating vocabulary, is the fast track to a fertile, nourishing culture in which innovation and creativity can thrive.

CHAPTER 8

Say It with Feeling: The Principles of Rhetorical Persuasion

There is no institution devised by man which the power of speech has not helped us to establish.[1]

As well as clarity and meaningfulness, there is another quality of language that's crucial to propagating the culture of a PROGRESSIVE ORGANISATION – its rhetorical power. Unfortunately, 'rhetoric' has become a dirty word. You'll see why, shortly. Yet rhetoric is all-pervasive in organisational communication. You can't escape it. You may not even recognise it. Rhetoric, as metaphor, is so ingrained in the English language it's easy to miss it. But there it is – all the time – conditioning people's minds, exerting an invisible influence on their thoughts and feelings.

Instead of allowing rhetoric to work stealthily, the time has come for Principled Persuaders to bring it out into the open and reinstate it as a force for good. The benefits of doing this are threefold:

1. It will become obvious what the real culture of the organisation is, and whether its rhetoric needs to change.
2. Rhetorical techniques can be deployed to stimulate dialogue throughout the organisation and improve the quality of discussions.
3. Rhetoric's ability to address itself to the emotional sensibilities of individuals can be used to increase empathy.

So let's clarify. What is rhetoric? Where did it come from? What is its story? How did it become such a negative word? And why, when there is now more

---

1   Isocrates (436–338 BC).

communication in the world than at any time in human history, are the skills of rhetoric so sadly neglected by all but a few?

The Roots of Rhetoric

The oldest essay ever discovered on effective public speaking was written around 3000 BC. Inscribed on parchment, it was addressed to Kagemni, the eldest son of the Pharaoh, Huni. Persuasive language has long been a skill essential to governance. During the fifth century BC, Tisias in Sicily, then his pupil Gorgias, are the first known teachers of rhetorical techniques. When rhetoric was introduced into Athens it became a hot topic, the latest craze. People were excited about this new way of looking at communication. Like fans of the latest iPhone, they queued up to get access to this dazzling verbal technology.

Something of the buzz it caused is captured in one of Plato's dialogues[2] where he imagines Gorgias debating rhetoric with Socrates, surrounded by an attentive audience. Asked whether rhetoric is all about persuasion, Gorgias agrees and defines its role as: 'To persuade people in the kind of mass meetings which happen in law courts and so on: and I think its province is right and wrong'. Socrates isn't satisfied. He thinks rhetoric misleads people and asks ironically: 'Do you think that when rhetoricians speak, they want what's best for their audience? Do you think they intend to have the effect of perfecting their fellow citizens?' Socrates obviously doesn't think so. Yet, he is prepared to admit that persuasion is justified if: 'We ... devote all our own and our community's energies towards ensuring the presence of justice and self-discipline, and so guaranteeing happiness', adding: 'rhetoric ... should only ever be used in the service of right'.

Isocrates, who ran a school of rhetoric in Athens, agreed. He could see how all around the city a small number of professional blackmailers were at work, extorting money by threatening lawsuits and using rhetorical skills to win them. It was clear to him that the persuasive powers of rhetoric should be used to achieve social progress. He said:

> because there is born in us the power to persuade each other and to
> show ourselves whatever we wish, we have not only escaped from

---

2   See the discussion in Plato, *Gorgias*, trans. Robin Waterfield (Oxford World Classic Edition, 2008), 7–27.

> *living as brutes, but also by coming together have founded cities and*
> *set up laws and invented arts.*[3]

For Isocrates, rhetoric was a discipline that could promote democracy, free speech and human rights.

In another part of the city, a young man called Aristotle was drafting his book, *The Art of Rhetoric*. His central insight was that to be effective, persuasion has to engage the emotions. The orator must understand what emotions are and what happens when people feel them. Effective persuasion, he said, is based on three elements: a credible source, clearly stated arguments and an appeal to emotions. He argued that the aim of persuasion should be to create an increase in happiness defined as 'prosperity combined with virtue; or as independence of life; or as the secure enjoyment of the maximum of pleasure; or as a good condition of property and body'.

Arguments over the virtues and vices of rhetoric are symbolised by the position of two statues in the temple at Athens. The goddess of persuasion, Peitho, stood alongside Aphrodite, the embodiment of love, beauty, pleasure and procreation. Why? Because the goddess of persuasion was not just associated with eloquence, but with seduction and rape. Rhetoric's capacity to be used for good or evil ends was recognised from the very beginning. That made it even more important that rhetoricians, like doctors, should be trained to use their skills for the common good.

Rhetoric in Rome

The virtuous qualities of rhetoric were strongly stressed by Marcus Tullius Cicero. By the first century BC, rhetoric was an intrinsic part of civil government. Lawyer and politician, Cicero believed in human rights and the brotherhood of man. He credited the development of civilisation to the power of persuasion. He described a time 'when men wandered at large in the field like animals' until leaders came along and 'transformed them from wild savages into a kind and gentle folk' by using 'reason and eloquence'.[4] He claimed: 'In every free

---

3   From Isocrates, *Antidosis*, quoted in Brian Vickers, *In Defence of Rhetoric* (Clarendon Paperbacks, 2002), 10.

4   From Cicero's first book on rhetoric, *De Inventione* [On Invention], written around 84 BC, quoted in Vickers, *In Defence of Rhetoric*, 10.

nation, and most of all in communities which have attained the enjoyment of peace and tranquillity, this one art [rhetoric] has always flourished'.[5]

About 100 years later, a teacher called Quintilian sat down to write a textbook on rhetoric. Running to around 200,000 words in 12 volumes, his *Institutes of Rhetoric* was a magisterial survey of rhetoric in all its aspects, giving the most comprehensive coverage of the subject to be produced in the classical era. He placed rhetoric at the centre of what it means to live a good life. The aspiring orator should learn how to use language in the service of ethical objectives. Aspiring orators should receive an education that broadens their minds and helps them see the close link between rhetoric and ethics. He urged the orators of the future to 'consider how honourable is the end which they claim to attain, and that no labour should be spared when such a reward is in view'.[6] He saw the harm rhetoric could do in the wrong hands, but argued that rejecting rhetoric for that reason was like refusing to eat because food can make you ill.

Rhetoric Rediscovered

Following the decline of the Roman Empire many classical texts fell into oblivion. Medieval scholars had only a partial and fragmentary view of the original theories of rhetoric. The texts on rhetoric they produced were as likely to bewilder as enlighten. The discipline was broken up into pieces and absorbed into other fields such as logic, theology, moral philosophy and the study of poetic forms. It was severed from its roots in human psychology and became a system of rules and verbal tricks. The persuasiveness of rhetoric was enlisted for personal purposes, for example, writing letters requesting jobs or money from powerful people. Knowledge of rhetoric was seen as essential for getting on in society. So it remained important for the educated classes to have a good grounding in its techniques.

To get some idea of how thorough this grounding was, here's a description of a scene in a London schoolyard in 1170, recorded by a Mr William Fitzstephen:[7]

> *The scholars dispute, some in demonstrative rhetoric, others in dialectic. Some hurtle enthymemes,*[8] *others with greater skill employ*

---

5   From Cicero, *De Oratore* [*On Rhetoric*], 55 BC, quoted in Vickers, *In Defence of Rhetoric*, 8.
6   From Quintilian's *Institutes of Oratory* (Henry G. Bohn, 1856).
7   Nicholas Orme, *English Schools in the Middle Ages* (Methuen, 1973).
8   An enthymeme is a maxim followed by an explanation. For example: 'There is no man among us all who is free'. 'For we are all slaves to money or chance'. An example of a

perfect syllogisms. Boys of different schools strive against each other in verse, or contend concerning the principles of grammar, or the rules concerning past and future. There are others who employ the old art of the crossroads in epigrams, rhymes and meter.

Pretty impressive, especially as these scholars were boys aged between 12 and 14.

In 1421, a complete copy of Quintilian's great work was found, covered in mould and dust, at the bottom of a tower in the Abbey of St Gall. More discoveries followed, including Cicero's and Aristotle's writings on rhetoric. The subject became a hot topic once again. Around 2,000 books were written on the art of rhetoric between 1400 and 1700 AD and read by several million people throughout Europe. Alongside training in Latin, rhetoric was firmly established in the school curriculum. In 1599 the Jesuits issued their blueprint for education, the 'Ratio Studiorum',[9] which went into 134 editions in 45 countries. It ensured millions of schoolboys in Catholic Europe would study rhetoric until the eighteenth century.

In Protestant England, the new grammar schools provided intense training in rhetoric. Children were taught how to construct a good speech, invent variations on a theme, play with word sounds and puns, argue both sides of a question, enlist metaphors to decorate a text and similes to point a moral. They read Cicero and Quintilian and learnt lots of different maxims from a book called *Wise Sayings for Young People*. The result was that rhetoric was in the bloodstream of the educated classes. For those who went to university, rhetoric remained part of the core curriculum, alongside grammar and logic, until the end of the eighteenth century.

As the English language expanded its vocabulary, rhetoric's social role was to provide a way of constructing powerful, meaningful texts that added enormously to the development of human understanding. What's more, Renaissance humanists, like their classical predecessors, saw rhetorical communication as a way of bringing people together, promoting harmony and love. Rhetoric in Britain reached its high point during the sixteenth and seventeenth centuries. In this pre-scientific age, rhetoric could still be seen as the application of intelligence, working on rational principles, to create language that is clear in meaning and effective in its appeal to the emotions.

---

syllogism is: 'All men are mortal; Greeks are men; therefore Greeks are mortal'.
9   The full name of the document was 'Ratio atque Studiorum Societatis Jesu' [A Systematic Plan for Jesuit Education].

Rhetoric's Rejection

It wasn't to last. Already in 1543, a professor of rhetoric at the University of Paris had mounted an attack on the classical works of rhetoric. He said the idea that rhetoricians could be virtuous as well as eloquent was 'useless and stupid'. Peter Ramus,[10] as he was known in Britain, separated rhetoric from the reasoning processes that had been so important to its classical integrity and assigned them to 'dialectic' (logic). Rhetoric, as a discipline, was hollowed out and left with verbal ornamentation. It took some time for this idea to reach Britain, but sure enough, by the late seventeenth century, it was plain that rhetoric's status as an art based on reason, as well as the emotions, was on the wane.

The new scientists hated it. They wanted language that was grounded in hard facts not fancies. The Royal Society of London advocated a 'close, naked, natural way of speaking, positive expressions, clear sense, a native easiness, bringing all things as near the mathematical plainness' as possible. It rejected all 'swellings of style'.[11] The art of eloquence was assigned to the realm of poetry and literature, and banished from the communication of important scientific discoveries.[12]

Nevertheless, rhetoric continued to be taught in British universities. In Edinburgh, a young Adam Smith set out the idea of 'New Rhetoric'. He taught how to adapt style to different subjects and drew on examples from classical and English literature. His new approach assigned argument to dialectic and presented rhetoric as a means of persuasion ideally suited to praising or condemning particular points of view. Yet rhetoric's flame as an instrument of social progress had not flickered out entirely. Smith's friend, Professor Hugh Blair, said: 'As society improves and flourishes, men acquire more influence over one another by means of reasoning and discourse'. He positioned the art of communication at the centre of intellectual life: 'To speak, to write perspicuously and agreeably, with purity, with grace and strength, are attainments of the utmost consequence to all who propose, either by speech or writing, to address the public.' According to Blair, if you can't explain a subject clearly, you probably don't understand it well enough – a precept just as relevant today.[13]

---

10 His French name was Pierre de la Ramée (1515–1572) and his book was called *Institutes of Dialectic*.

11 From Thomas Sprat, *History of the Royal Society* (1667), quoted by Ian Simpson Ross in *The Life of Adam Smith* (Oxford University Press, 2010), 81.

12 However, as we shall see later, rhetoric became part of scientific discourse. It was unavoidable as scientists often explained their work to non-scientists by using metaphorical language.

13 Quotations from Hugh Blair, *Lectures on Rhetoric and Belles Lettres* (1803 edition [1783]).

Rhetoric struggled on through the nineteenth century, but despite its survival as part of literary studies, elocution, political and legal oratory and preaching, it had lost its status as a force for good. By the first half of the twentieth century it had all but disappeared from the educational system. The art of clear expressive speech, of being confident in front of an audience, of structuring arguments in the most powerful way, of spotting weaknesses in other people's arguments, no longer seemed to be valued as qualities all educated people should have. Instead, as you'll see in the next chapter, the skills of rhetoric were reserved for powerful and influential people seeking to impose their vision of the world on others.

Now, in the twenty-first century, with the mighty engines of global communication running at full blast, it's time to rediscover the fundamentals of rhetoric and reinstate it as a force for good, especially in organisations. Rhetoric's power to contribute to a good life at work rests on three distinct but interrelated roles – as metaphor, dialogue and empathy.

Rhetoric as Metaphor

The English language is an ocean of metaphor. You're swimming in it every day. Most of the time you're not even aware of it. The effect of this daily soaking in metaphor is to condition minds. It has an effect similar to brainwashing in that you end up making assumptions, led on by language. That's because language is never neutral. It's always pointing us in one direction or another. It primes us constantly. What's more, metaphors draw on emotions and intellect in equal measure, making them a powerful force for good or evil. That's why, as a first step towards reinventing rhetoric, all organisations should analyse their use of metaphor. It will tell them what kind of internal culture they have.

Metaphor acts as a bridge over which meaning can cross. It links two separate ideas and transfers meaning from one to the other. It comes in the form of simile – 'she was frisky as a lamb', metonym – 'The Head is in charge of the school' and figures of speech such as 'he kept shooting questions at me'. Some linguists believe that metaphor is wired into your brain from early childhood. You associate freedom with space as you begin to crawl around; progress is linked to forward movement; as you push yourself up and stand on your own two feet, 'up' is forever associated with success and 'down' with failure; when you grip an object to explore it, 'gripping' and 'grasping' become metaphors for understanding. Whether this is all true or not, it's certain that metaphors bubble up in human communication as naturally as water from a spring.

Every now and then, a new wave of metaphors crashes into the English language, usually derived from the latest technologies. Ancient metaphors of nature and the body have been supplemented over time with metaphors of cultivation, clocks, machines, evolution, space travel, computers, the Internet, genetics, and so on and on. These new metaphors enrich the language enormously and help everyone get to grips with new concepts by relating them to those they already understand.

When they've been around long enough, they become so-called 'dead metaphors'. That's why you don't notice them; they've stopped moving. If you say, 'he's fallen into a depression' or 'inflation is eating into my savings' or 'her cancer finally caught up with her', you are using intensely metaphorical language. According to some experts,[14] this unconscious use of metaphor means that there is a conditioning effect: certain social practices are reinforced; biases lie latent and unchallenged. For example, saying 'I don't buy that idea' reinforces a consumerist approach to intellectual development; you shop around for the ideas you like.

It's very difficult to unpick all this; especially as such language is inextricably woven into our thoughts and feelings. But it is possible to adopt a conscious approach to the use of metaphor in organisations. Software can be used to analyse the metaphorical content in your organisation's streams of communication. Some researchers have begun to explore the use of metaphors in organisations. With a database of 100,000 texts, one piece of research[15] has revealed 11 commonly used metaphorical clusters, namely: war and conflict, animal and human life, plants, machinery and mechanics, illness and remedies, eating and drinking, journeys, navigation, games and sports, hunting, building.

They're all too familiar. 'We need to hit our targets but we've got some distance to go. Sales are reasonably healthy but competitors are picking all the low hanging fruit. We need to swallow some extra costs and dig deep into our promotional budget. Let's put them under pressure until we've won this battle. Then we can set a new course for the market by introducing some game changing innovations.' A little exaggerated, possibly, but you get the idea.

In the PROGRESSIVE ORGANISATION every attempt will be made to introduce metaphors appropriate to growth, creativity and innovation. An organisation whose leaders speak in terms of war, conflicts and battles, sets up different

---

14 See Andrew Goatley, *Washing the Brain: Metaphor and Hidden Ideology* (John Benjamin, 2007).

15 Hanna Skorczynska, *Metaphor Use and Discourse Specialisation* (2010), quoted in Honesto Herrera-Soler and Michael White (eds), *Metaphor and Mills: Figurative Language in Business and Economics* (De Gruyter Mouton, 2012).

standards of behaviour from those that use metaphors from the world of sports or games. Communication that presents an organisation's development as a continuous journey will evoke a different response from that which sees it as a race to the finish. Metaphors of nourishment, growth, fertility, cross-pollination, seeding, nurturing and so on, are more likely to foster a creative culture than metaphors of the machine and engineered systems.

Rhetoric as Dialogue

Totalitarian regimes hate the idea of open debate. Nor are authoritarian organisations too keen on promoting widespread and challenging conversations. Dialogue, open discussions and debate with well-presented arguments for and against, undermine command and control structures. Or at least that's how some senior managers, who have grown up within hierarchical systems, will see it. Yet the PROGRESSIVE ORGANISATION understands that tapping into 'the wisdom of crowds',[16] including its employees, will make a significant contribution to its ability to survive and prosper in the twenty-first century.

Quite apart from its function as expressive language, classical rhetoric embraced the idea of rigorous discussion and argument as central to establishing the right way forward. Students of rhetoric were taught how to take a single question, and then present arguments on both sides. The challenge was to find equally convincing points to prove the case one way or the other. This remains the basis of the Anglo-Saxon legal system. Behind this process lies a deep psychological principle that you will read more about in the next chapter; what is real and true depends on perceptions.

Humanity will probably never be in a position where all judgements can be made scientifically, based on incontestable facts. Most decisions are judgement calls. Up to the point of making the decision it's vital to gather as much accurate information as possible and then assemble arguments for and against certain ways of proceeding. But even then, uncertainty, ambiguity, ambivalence and fear of risk all have an impact on the quality of decisions. The PROGRESSIVE ORGANISATION takes the view that the quality of its decisions depends on the extent to which it can stimulate high quality discussion and conversations at all levels across all disciplines. This continuous process of argument and debate, punctuated by decisions at key moments, is the best way known to man of making real progress.

---

16 James Surowiecki, *The Wisdom of Crowds* (Abacus, 2005), explores how to aggregate and analyse information from many diverse sources.

What's the alternative? As in the past, to leave it to a few top people and their advisers? That's not a sensible path to follow in the twenty-first century when lines of communication, and the methods to analyse the information in them, are proliferating. To say the world is 'multi-dimensional' sounds a bit like a cliché. But it is true that more dimensions are opening up all the time in the form of multiple, well informed perspectives. This kind of world needs continuous, multi-sided argument to work through the alternatives. You could call this process 'polyphonic dialogue'.

For many people, this idea of continuous, multi-sided debate, resolved peacefully by decisions that win support, is the best way to make social progress. One such is Jurgen Habermas[17] who outlined the 'rules of discourse' in society as follows:

1.   Every subject with the competence to speak and act is allowed to take part in the discourse.
2.   a) Everyone is allowed to question any assertion whatever.
      b) Everyone is allowed to introduce any assertion into the discourse.
      c) Everyone is allowed to express their attitudes, desires and needs.
3.   No speaker should be prevented from taking part as per 1 and 2.

Following such rules can be very difficult in organisations. A lot of things get in the way of mature discourse; groupthink, embarrassment, dominant characters, fear of consequences of raising challenges and so on. One of the biggest difficulties of all is a lack of practice in expressing ideas clearly and effectively, and analysing arguments. That's why more employees need to be trained in communication skills. The new, more educated workforce of the twenty-first century is capable of engaging in mature and reasoned discussion if enabled to do so.

One eminent thinker, John Stuart Mill, set out some time ago how challenging conversations can benefit the individual's ability to learn and think. In *On Liberty* (1859), he says:

> *the only way in which a human being can make some approach to knowing the whole of a subject is by hearing what can be said about it by persons of every variety of opinion ... knowing that he has*

---

17 Born in 1929, Jurgen Habermas is an influential German philosopher whose work covers epistomology, philosophy of language, political and constitutional theory, ethics and aesthetics. The rules of discourse are from *Moral Consciousness and Communication Action* (1989).

sought for objections and difficulties instead of avoiding them, and has shut out no light which can be thrown upon the subject from any quarter.[18]

This message will resonate loudly with leaders in PROGRESSIVE ORGANISATIONS.

Rhetoric as Empathy

If the rational aim of organisational rhetoric is to present arguments clearly and effectively, then its emotional aim is to encourage higher levels of empathy throughout the workforce. Empathy, your ability to identify with others, to 'put yourself in their shoes', is central to an ethical and happy life. It is an essential part of your emotional intelligence, helping you to achieve your goals without harming others, and sensitising you to other people's emotions.

When, back in the sixteenth and seventeenth centuries, scientists tried to shunt rhetoric into the intellectual sidings, they found themselves unable to avoid metaphorical language themselves. Neither could they answer the question 'what does it mean to live a good life?' Instead it was rhetoric, finding expression in a rich and comprehensive literature, that helped provide the answers. The poetry and fiction of the nineteenth and twentieth centuries allowed people to reconstruct in their own imaginations the emotional experiences of others. They opened windows to a wider world for millions, and helped them grow as individuals.

Rhetoric in organisations has a similar literary function. The stories it tells, through narratives and metaphors, allow employees to see completely different perspectives from their own. The experiences gained through exposure to the stories of others, in Martha Nussbaum's words, 'not only increase our understanding of our own emotional geography', they help to keep 'our personality in an open and permeable condition'.[19] If organisations can be thought of as having a collective imagination, then rhetoric, through powerfully expressed stories, has a central role to play in enabling that imagination to develop creatively.

By increasing levels of empathy in the workforce, rhetoric shows its close link with ethics. Indeed, some thinkers have focused on empathetic relationships between people as the foundation of ethical behaviour. Martin

---

18 John Stuart Mill, *On Liberty* (Cosimo Classics, 2005 [1859]), 25.
19 Martha Nussbaum, *Upheavals of Thought: The Intelligence of Emotions* (Cambridge University Press. 2005), 244.

Buber,[20] for example, in 'I and Thou' (1923), said there were two fundamental interpersonal relationships. In the 'I-it' relationship, the 'I' is careful to present just one aspect of itself to the other person, what you might call a 'front'; this 'I' sees the other person as a means to an end, someone who's useful. This type of instrumental relationship is widespread in organisations. The other, more enriching relationship is 'I-thou' where the 'I' opens up to the other person, shows all sides of its personality and engages in communication which is mutually beneficial. It is this type of relationship that builds strong communities, said Buber.

PROGRESSIVE ORGANISATIONS should use the literary qualities of rhetoric to boost the number of 'I-thou' relationships between employees. This is not straightforward. That's because everyone that works in organisations has learned a kind of 'emotional grammar'. You have to mind your emotional 'Ps' and 'Qs'. Many emotions are hidden, even repressed. Yet the presence of stories allows people to share their feelings about certain situations without exposing themselves too much. The experiences are objectified, made less personal. This is how soap operas and other dramas on television contribute to social change. They allow people to reflect aloud on many issues that were previously taboo or hard to talk about. Stories that present real-life dilemmas and difficulties in organisations have the same effect.

Principled Persuaders, using the Happiness and Harm profiles put together from continuous feedback data, are in the best position to assess the emotional sensibilities of their organisation's workforce. The rhetoric of the organisation needs to be tuned into those emotional needs.

The Principles of Rhetorical Persuasion

Instead of continuing to see rhetoric as misleading puffery, it's time to reinvent it as a timeless skill for organisations to use to the benefit of all employees. The rhetorical approach nourishes internal culture through expressive metaphors; it promotes dialogue and reasoned arguments; it increases empathy between individuals. In the PROGRESSIVE ORGANISATION, rhetoric is not seen as an enemy of truth, but as the means to opening up multiple discourses, allowing new truths to emerge in the form of creative and innovative ideas. Here are the principles on which the rhetorical approach is based.

---

20 Martin Buber (1878–1965) was a Jewish philosopher born in Vienna and raised in the Ukraine. He believed authenticity and responsiveness are only present in the 'I-thou' relationship.

Principle 1: Acknowledge rhetoric as a force for good

Throw away outdated notions and embrace the ancient skills of rhetoric as a means to social and institutional progress. Accept that rhetoric already exists in organisations, whether you like it or not, and that it needs to be managed to the benefit of all. The essence of the rhetorical approach is a fundamental concern for the opinions, values and emotions of employees.

Principle 2: Determine the right metaphors to use

The metaphorical language of the organisation sets the tone of its culture. Analyse the current use of metaphor; evaluate it against how you want the organisation to develop; consciously choose a metaphorical language that will help you redescribe the organisation; introduce it into all forms of communication.

Principle 3: Use rhetorical techniques to stimulate debate

Rhetoric is ideally suited to encouraging everyone to put forward well-articulated views in an atmosphere of collaboration and mutual respect. A structured approach to reasoned argument in meetings and conversations would boost productivity and innovation. It's also more challenging and interesting for participants.

Principle 4: Use rhetorical narrative to increase empathy

Stories educate, entertain and persuade. The literary quality of organisational communication should be founded on stories that allow employees to reconstruct the experiences of others in their imaginations. This means sharing working experiences of all kinds, from all parts and levels of the organisation.

Principle 5: Introduce training in rhetorical techniques

Sadly, most schools do not teach communication skills well. Until they do, organisations need to expand training in public speaking, structuring and presenting arguments, and expressive writing. What's more useless than a mumbling manager in the twenty-first century?

I hope you agree by now that rhetoric can be a powerful force for good in organisations. Principled Persuaders won't keep the art of rhetoric to themselves, but spread it as widely as possible throughout the organisation. With appropriate training, many employees will see rhetoric, in the form of more effective communication, as helpful to achieving their goals.

Yet there's a dark side to rhetoric when it's in the hands of people seeking to control rather than liberate. That's what we need to look at next. How can you tell the difference between principled, ethical persuasion and propaganda?

How can you be certain that your communication programmes are following the path towards truth, not falsity? And what is truth in the twenty-first century anyway?

CHAPTER 9

Tell the Truth: The Principles of Truthful Persuasion

Once to every man and nation comes the moment to decide,
In the strife of truth with falsehood, for the good or evil side.[1]

A mixture of fear and contempt describes the attitude of the elite towards the 'masses' for most of the nineteenth and twentieth centuries. The fear stemmed from what might happen once the masses were exposed to new ideas in newspapers and popular literature. The contempt flowed from an innate sense of superiority. These attitudes were deeply entrenched in British society, well into the 1970s, when everything began to change.

The arrival of cheap books, periodicals and newspapers, followed by cinemas, radios and televisions, made it possible for ordinary people to discover new worlds. At the same time, it provided more opportunities for the elite to gain control over the masses using the dark side of rhetoric, propaganda. For most of the twentieth century it looked as though propaganda was winning the battle for the hearts and minds of the people. Instead, what happened was an unprecedented opening up of new perspectives.

As the twentieth century got underway, the coming together of new disciplines like psychology, psychoanalysis, statistical measurement of intelligence, social Darwinism and eugenics inspired elites to believe that it was possible to create a more ideal society. They called it 'social engineering', a metaphor from the age of machines. The remnants of this way of thinking are still with us. As you will see, attempts are still being made to change the way people think and behave through different forms of propaganda.

Take the world of work for example. Even now, in the twenty-first century, leaders in many organisations remain fearful of providing too much information to their employees. They either don't trust them with it or feel they don't need to know. What's more, by using Motivational Communication,

---

1   Robert Lowell, *The Present Crisis* (1845).

managers with the command and control mindset can all too easily slip into propaganda mode. So, in ENGINEERED ORGANISATIONS, you have a recipe for keeping employees in the dark about the really serious issues while pushing them along with forms of communication encouraging them to 'go the extra mile' or show 'greater commitment' or 'engagement'.

The switch to Principled Persuasion acknowledges that employees don't want to be motivated, or engaged. They want the freedom to flourish as individuals, to learn, to be challenged, to have a real say in what happens around them. Too many employees are still denied these experiences. That's why, in this chapter, you're going to read how the elite looked down on the masses and, in some ways, still does; how techniques of propaganda spread across the world; how the advent of mass media was equated with brainwashing; and, wonderfully, how the elite was proved spectacularly wrong as new perspectives were shared across the world by ordinary people, leading to a new age of tolerance and individualism.

This is a story that twenty-first-century organisations need to take to heart. For most of the last century, organisations trudged slowly and reluctantly behind the mighty forces of social change, forced to keep up by the sergeants of legislation. The time has come for leaders in organisations to abandon propagandistic ways of communication. Let go of 'visions' and 'missions', and become truthful in the presentation of organisational successes and failures, as well as future difficulties and opportunities. Share more with employees, and you will be rewarded by a surge of innovation and creativity that benefits everyone. That's been the story of society – it should also be the story of the PROGRESSIVE ORGANISATION.

What Do *They* Know?

As soon as papers and books began to fly off the presses in volume, the elite started to worry about their potential to sway the minds of ordinary folk. Leading Victorian critic, Matthew Arnold, said:

> *Plenty of people will try to give the masses, as they call them, an intellectual food prepared and adapted in the way they think proper for the actual condition of the masses. The ordinary popular literature is an example of this way of working on the masses. Plenty of people will try to indoctrinate the masses with the set of*

ideas and judgments constituting the creed of their own profession or party.[2]

This was a theme set to recur over and over again in the century to follow. Attitudes hardened. In 1923, military strategist John Fuller distinguished between super-men, the masters, and super-monkeys, the slaves. He saw the latter as 'mentally challenged, naturally fearful, and tending to the feminine'.[3] In 1933, Sigmund Freud, in a letter to Einstein, wrote:

That men are divided into leaders and the led is but another manifestation of their inborn and irremediable inequality ... men should be at greater pains than heretofore to form a superior class of independent thinkers, unamenable to intimidation and fervent in the quest of truth, whose function it would be to guide the masses dependent on their lead.[4]

In 1932, Cambridge academic Queenie Leavis complained:

Journalists, advertising agents, editors of magazines and popular authors were naturally the first to discover that it is more profitable to make use of man's suggestibility as a herd animal than to approach the reader as if he were what used to be called 'the thinking man'.[5]

In 1941, poet and critic T.S. Eliot felt he needed an interpreter to help him address the masses on the radio. 'Where are the men who are intelligent enough to understand your thinking, but yet superficial enough to be able to translate it?' He thought his talks would be 'unintelligible to the mob'.[6]

In 1954, English critic J.B. Priestley, on a trip to the United States, coined the term 'Admass'. He defined it as:

the whole system of an increasing productivity, plus inflation, plus a rising standard of material living, plus high-pressure advertising and

---

2   Matthew Arnold, *Culture and Anarchy* (Cambridge University Press, 1950 [1859]), 69–70.

3   Lawrence Freedman, *Strategy: A History* (Oxford University Press, 2013), 132.

4   In a letter from Freud to Einstein, 1933, quoted in Steven Bartlett, *The Pathology of Man: A Study of Human Evil* (Charles C. Thomas, 2005), 82.

5   Q.D. Leavis, *Fiction and the Reading Public* (Chatto & Windus, 1965 [1932]), 192.

6   T.S. Eliot to Philip Mairet, 1941, quoted in Stefan Collini, *Absent Minds: Intellectuals in Britain* (Oxford University Press, 2006), 314.

salesmanship, plus mass communication, plus cultural democracy and the creation of the mass mind, the mass man.[7]

In 1956, during the Suez crisis, MP Harold Nicolson wrote:

It is preferable that the general public should be unintellectual … they should spend much of their time, and relieve many internal tensions, by worrying about cricket matches rather than worrying about what is happening in Cairo or Tel Aviv.[8]

Looking back, it's obvious that what was missing was educational opportunity, not intelligence. The same point can be made about today's employees. What's missing is not a good strategic sense, or sound judgement, but the opportunity to be fully informed and educated. Some commercial secrets are necessary, obviously. But the default position should be to tell employees the truth about what's happening and provide them with the opportunities to learn more about all aspects of the organisation's work. Leaders who feel their ordinary employees haven't got what it takes to assess complex and uncertain situations follow directly in the footsteps of all those elites who felt most of the public were ignorant fools and did nothing to help them.

Propaganda Raises its Beastly Head

At first, as events unfolded in the first half of the twentieth century, fears that mass communication could unleash a monster were proved right. It was during the terrible bloodshed of the First World War that the word 'propaganda' began to be used to describe a systematic, manipulative process of persuasion. A secret bureau in London invented new techniques of propaganda, including distorting the news sent to the United States to encourage it to join in, and atrocity stories. It was claimed Germans were boiling down human bodies to make soap, cutting off children's hands, crucifying prisoners of war, even using priests as clappers in church bells: distasteful stuff, yet effective in appealing to the base emotions of hatred and fear. The beast, propaganda, was out of its cage and looking for more victims. It didn't have long to wait.

---

7   J.B. Priestley and J. Hawkes, *Journey Down a Rainbow* (1954), quoted in John Baxendale, *Priestley's England* (Manchester University Press, 2007), 177.
8   Collini, *Absent Minds*, 155.

When the war was over it became obvious how the truth had been distorted. Many Americans were shocked. Adolf Hitler was impressed. But was this just a wartime phenomenon? What about in peacetime? What you read in newspapers, was that the truth? A brilliant, young American journalist, Walter Lippman, decided to tell the public some home truths. In doing so he sparked off a major controversy. In his book, *Public Opinion*, he pointed out that every individual had a unique way of looking at things. One person's truth was another's falsehood. He described how many of the attitudes people form are based on mistaken perceptions and, sometimes, complete fictions. What matters, he argued, is not what the truth actually is, but what people think it is. Perceptions are reality. The real truth, if there is one, hardly matters: 'We shall assume that what each man does is based not on certain and direct knowledge, but on pictures made by himself or given to him'.[9]

Lippman's book was seen by some as an attack on the democratic ideal. It greatly offended those who felt well informed and able to make up their own minds on political and social matters. Yet it contained a real insight. Most people simply don't have time to make long and considered analyses of the issues of the day. They need news to be packaged up for them and made easily digestible. They rely on being told the truth. This puts a great deal of power into the hands of journalists and others who want to influence public opinion. People like PR man, Edward Bernays, who said:

> *The conscious and intelligent manipulation of the organised habits and opinions of the masses is an important element in democratic society.*[10]

The controversy over propaganda in the United States led to setting up the Institute for Propaganda Analysis in 1937. Its aim was to help the public recognise and neutralise the manipulative communication targeted at them.[11] It taught that there are seven common propaganda devices. It's worth checking your current communication programmes against this list.

---

9   Walter Lippman, *Public Opinion* (Free Press Paperbacks, 1997 [1922]), 16.

10   These were the opening words in Edward L. Bernays, *Propaganda* (Kennikat Press, 1972 [1928]). Bernays was Sigmund Freud's nephew.

11   The IPA's definition of propaganda was 'The expression of opinions or actions carried out deliberately, by individuals or groups, with a view to influencing the opinions or actions of other individuals or groups, for predetermined ends and through psychological manipulations'.

1.   Name-calling: from Nazis calling Jews 'sub-humans' to modern-day attacks on 'welfare scroungers' – name-calling is a sure sign of an appeal to prejudice.

2.   Glittering generalities: such high flown and meaningless phrases like 'we will be the best in everything we do'. 'Visions' and 'Missions' are full of glittering generalities.

3.   Transference: giving borrowed credibility to controversial or unpopular ideas: 'our management consultants recommended ...'

4.   Plain folks: 'I'm the CEO, but I'm just like you' – there he is, sleeves rolled up, perched on a desk to give an informal talk – be careful; it might be genuine or an attempt to soften people up for hard decisions.

5.   Card-stacking: this includes lies, distortions, oversimplifications, omissions. This is the cause of much distrust in organisations. It's hard to spot, but people often have an instinct for when they're not being told the true story.

6.   Bandwagon: everybody's doing it, so should you. Tell everyone an idea is popular and, you never know, it might become so. It's a popular technique in 'nudging', which you'll read about shortly.

7.   Emotional appeals: watch out for appeals to base emotions like fear, anger, hatred and so on.

Fantastically good advice, but it all faded into obscurity when the Second World War started. A torrent of propaganda swept across the globe. The Nazis got off to a fast start. Hitler was so impressed by British propaganda in the First World War he made it a cornerstone of his power. Utterly contemptuous of ordinary people's intelligence, he wrote in *Mein Kampf*: 'Because of the primitive simplicity of their minds' they would fall victim to the big lie because it 'would never come into their heads to fabricate colossal untruths, and they would not believe that others could have the impudence to distort the truth so infamously'. In 1933, propaganda chief Josef Goebbels set up the Ministry of Propaganda and Public Enlightenment. He said:

> *It would not be impossible to prove with sufficient repetition and psychological understanding of the people concerned that a square is in fact a circle. What after all are a square and a circle? They are mere words and words can be moulded until they clothe ideas in disguise.*[12]

---

12 Garth S. Jowett and Victoria O'Donnell, *Propaganda and Persuasion* (Sage Publications, 1992), 185.

Mass Manipulation by Mass Media?

Hitler's control of his population through propaganda was made easier by the rapid spread of cheap radios throughout the Fatherland. By the 1950s radio was the principal mass medium across the world and newspaper readerships were huge too. In Britain, 20 million people read the *Radio Times*, over 17 million the *News of the World* and 13 million the *People*. But it was the arrival of television that turned the power of mass media up to new levels. In 1953, 20 million people watched the coronation of Queen Elizabeth on just two million TV sets. By the 1980s, virtually every household had a set. This was a unique communication vehicle. It brought drama and excitement straight into people's living rooms every evening. During the 1960s, soaps like *Coronation Street* regularly attracted audiences of more than 20 million. Here was a medium capable of changing social customs, of influencing minds for better or worse.

By the 1950s, events seemed to be proving the wisdom of the maxim 'A lie can travel halfway around the world before the truth can get its boots on'. American adman, James Vicary, claimed he had arranged for the words EAT POPCORN and DRINK COKE to be flashed at 1/3,000th of a second during a movie. As a result, he said sales of Coke had gone up by 18.1 per cent and popcorn by 57.7 per cent. This apparent use of subliminal advertising provoked a furore. The worst predictions about sinister manipulation seemed to have come true. But it was a hoax. Vicary was lying. Yet, at the height of the media storm, 81 per cent of respondents in a poll believed subliminal advertising was current practice. The myth entered folklore and helped contribute to the suspicion that there were people out there determined to use ever more deceptive ways of selling products. Suspicions reinforced by Vance Packard, who, in *The Hidden Persuaders*, showed how admen were using the insights of psychiatry and the social sciences to influence choices. He said advertisers were exploiting people's deep psychological needs.

By the 1960s, fear of mass manipulation was broadening out into a widespread critique of propaganda as a form of social conditioning or brainwashing. In 1963, J.A.C. Brown published *Techniques of Persuasion* and pointed out that, in China and the Soviet Union, the words 'propaganda' and 'education' were interchangeable. Was this the case in the Western world? After all, he said, 'the prevailing ideology of any period will favour that of the ruling economic class'. He added:

> *Psychiatrists and teachers increasingly see the ideal of normality in*
> *'social adjustment', taking care not to enquire too carefully into the*
> *question 'Adjustment to what? And for what purpose?'*

In France, philosopher Jacques Ellul explained that propaganda is everywhere and 'an indispensable condition for the development of technical progress and the establishment of a technological civilisation'.[13] In his eyes, all mass communication, from teaching to advertising, is propaganda designed to protect the economic system. It channels people's thinking along certain lines. He described the process as 'slow, constant impregnation' of specific ideas that prompt specific actions, whether it be buying a product or accepting the need to go to work. He argued that there are manipulative people behind the scenes that have an interest in moving others in a particular direction and they will use all the communication skills in their power to achieve their objectives. These people are deeply cynical:

> *The true propagandist must be as cold, lucid and rigorous as*
> *a surgeon ... A propagandist who believes what he says and lets*
> *himself become a victim of his own game will have the same weakness*
> *as a surgeon who operates on a loved one.*

He was, perhaps, confusing the rhetorical power of language with propaganda. There was no conspiracy, just an unravelling of events during which people were, as ever, trying to live the best lives they could given the conditions they faced. In fact, far from being a vehicle for controlling minds, mass communication was opening them up. The advanced world was about to witness the greatest and fastest revolution in social attitudes in human history.

New Perspectives

At 3.32 p.m., on 15 July 1972, a prize-winning block of flats was blown up, to be followed by 32 others. Despite the architectural credentials of the Pruitt Igoe estate in St Louis, it was considered unfit for human habitation. This event has been named, perhaps slightly tongue-in-cheek, as the moment at which postmodernism took over from modernism. The Corbusier-inspired style of building that Pruitt Igoe represented was symbolic of an era in which

---

13   Jacque Ellul, *Propaganda: The Formation of Men's Attitudes* (Borzoi Books, 1965), x.

government officials and planners thought they knew best. The ruling elite had its own vision of how to regulate, direct and control the lives of ordinary people. Yet, as these flats tumbled to the ground, new ways of thinking were on the rise.

Like an exploding volcano, from the 1970s onwards, the diverse aspirations and desires of the masses burst through, what turned out to be, a thin crust of authoritarianism, to find expression in a multiplicity of views about the world and its values. The eruption that scattered so many values in all directions was an inevitable consequence of mass communications. For the first time, new ideas, fashions, music and portrayals of other people's ways of life could be instantly seen and heard by millions across the world. Government propaganda continued, but it was countered by what people saw for themselves on their screens: the brutal murders perpetrated in Vietnam; the terrible scenes of famine with close-ups of starving children, flies crawling across their parched lips; the shocking plays about poverty-stricken people who could be living in the flats just around the corner from you.[14]

People were forced to realise that their immediate environment, all the things they knew so well and took for granted, were just one manifestation of how it was in the world; that there were endless different cultures, sets of circumstances and different ways of evaluating what had seemed to be fixed and certain truths. Mass communication speeded up the process whereby different views of what was right and wrong in the world began to collide. The result was not fusion, but confusion. How on earth could you make sense of what was going on?

Enter the postmodernists,[15] who during their period of greatest influence in the 1970s and 1980s said that there is no sense to be made of it. Instead,

---

14 *Cathy Come Home* is a prime example. First broadcast by the BBC on 16 November 1966 it was watched by 12 million people. It was a searing portrayal of the difficulties of a young woman who became homeless and had her children taken away from her.

15 Postmodernism, as a way of thinking, has many critics. Here's how *the Oxford Companion of Philosophy* defines it: 'A family-resemblance term deployed in a variety of contexts ... for things which seem to be related – if at all – by a laid back pluralism of styles and a vague desire to have done with the pretensions of high-modernist culture'. In the context of this book, I use 'postmodernism' as a convenient label for describing the era in which it became possible for individuals to assert their own version of reality, the world as they see it, and be listened to seriously. However, the study of postmodernism should come with a health warning. It is not for the faint-hearted. Writers like Jean-Francois Lyotard, Jacques Derrida, Michel Foucault, Roland Barthes, Jean Baudrillard (notice the French connection?) invented a whole new universe of jargon. Even some of the books that set out to explain postmodernism are hard to understand. Here's an example of what you might expect: 'At the postmodern level of analysis the focus is upon "the rules grounded in practices which precede subjectivity", which is essentially the structuralist attack upon the philosophy of consciousness'. John Hassard and Martin Parker, *Postmodernism and Organizations* (Sage Publications, 1993), 2.

you have to see the world as a chameleon-like entity, full of illusions and deceptions, where truth is relative. They said that, in the realm of values, it is impossible to prove objectively that one set of values is better than another, so you should not impose your values on anyone else; instead you should tolerate points of view that conflict with yours; there are no absolutes, no standards that can be objectively justified; you are a product of your personal history; your beliefs are utterly contingent on the cultures in which you grew up and now live.

Challenges to relativism came fast and furious. Concepts like freedom, justice and human rights were universals, surely? If there is a clear case of somebody being imprisoned unjustly, it can't be right to say that it's just a matter of perceptions. More importantly, if you regard all values as relative, if you stand aside from committing yourself to deciding what is true or false, then you contradict a deep inner need to live within a framework of values that makes sense to you. You can't float freely through a value-neutral world. You have to be anchored in a set of beliefs that you regard as true, not just for you, but also for the world in which you live.

The arguments kick-started a rethink on long-held social attitudes. The decades of the 1980s and 1990s saw many people across the world revise their attitudes and behaviour towards women, gays, black communities, the mentally ill and the disabled. Much derided, 'politically correct' language came in to replace sexist, racist and other insulting words often used unconsciously by many ordinary people. In education, the traditional curriculum was now seen as hidebound with old prejudices and inbuilt biases and revised. In literature there were those who questioned the validity of traditional judgements about what was worth reading. Environmental activism got under way. And many started to question the very idea of 'progress' in the shape of economic growth and material prosperity. They saw the whole ideological system, politics, education, religion and the world of work, all marching in lock step towards some distant goal.

The Internet's arrival in the 1990s opened a Pandora's box of information, as well as different values and cultures. Who could be certain of picking a way through the various truths and falsehoods now available to people of all nations, classes and ages, at the touch of a button? For individuals, seated in front of their screens, it's possible to 'pick and mix' aspects of the world they find most appealing to them. If they wish, they can construct their own realities, their own bespoke framework of truths and falsehoods.

Mass Deconstruction

By the turn of the new millennium, critics of the public's intelligence had fallen silent. A new orthodoxy, based on free consumer choices and voices, was setting in. The mass audiences of the second half of the twentieth century had disappeared. Like a meteor entering the atmosphere, this apparently solid mass had shattered into fragments. New technologies of communication made it possible to reach smaller and smaller audiences. Categories of upper, middle and working class gave way to a bewildering variety of smaller groups. Are you an 'affluent grey' or an 'emergent service worker'? Perhaps you're 'an aspiring single' currently working in the 'precariat'? In the twenty-first century, society will continue to morph, changing shape like swirling cloud.

Diversity of lifestyle is the new norm. The collective voice has all but faded away, hanging on mostly in the public sector. Society has deconstructed itself into individuals that want more opportunities to live the way they want to live; to say, 'it's none of your business' to anyone who tries to impose their version of the truth on them. A constant flux of people from all over the world, sometimes moving through, sometimes settling, has brought different customs and ways of thinking into this new society. There has been a massive increase in consumer choice, allowing people to define themselves in ever more subtle ways.[16] In education, the comprehensive model is slowly giving way to a variety of educational structures in which the organising principle is that of differentiation. In the political arena, the trend is towards devolving power downwards from the centre. Individually tailored healthcare is on its way. In advanced countries, the future is going to be all about how to cater for the individual, not the masses. This would all seem to leave little room for propaganda. But it's still there.

Propaganda in Organisations

Many organisations are struggling to keep up with social change, at least as far as their employees are concerned. Weighed down by histories, hierarchies and

---

16 Not everyone is happy with this flourishing of choice: for example, take this comment in an essay entitled 'A Post-Fordist Consumption Norm? Social Fragmentation, Individualisation and New Inequalities': 'In the postmodern context there is no need to provide reasons to consume since consumerism has become the raison d'être for everything else leading to a playful and self-complacent aesthetic'. Benito Alonso, Luis Enrique and Miguel Martinez-Lucio, *Employment Relations in a Changing Society: Assessing the Post-Fordist Paradigm* (Palgrave Macmillan, 2005).

vested interests, it's hard for them to move as quickly as society itself. At work, employees experience a different world from the one outside. The degree of control that's exerted over many employees would simply not be acceptable in private life. The people you're surrounded by at work, particularly managers, are not often those with whom you would choose to spend your leisure time. You're lucky if that's not the case. Your chance to have a real say in what's going on is strictly limited. At work, employees don't get to vote for their leaders.

Instead they are bombarded with Motivational Communication. They're coaxed to share prescribed values; they're asked to find significance in the motherhood and apple pie vocabulary of vision and mission statements; they're given pats on the back for hard work as well as games and days out, maybe. These relics of the paternalistic system are still alive and kicking.

They were already worrying about all this back in the 1950s. According to William H. Whyte,[17] for example, employees of big companies were victims of new mind control techniques. He described how organisations were busily cultivating corporate automata that left any vestiges of individuality they had at home, well before they reached the office door. They were tested to see if they would fit the holes they were destined to fill: 'Now in regular use are tests which tell in decimal figures a man's degree of radicalism versus conservatism, his practical judgment, his social judgment, the amount of perseverance he has, his stability, his contentment index'.[18] It's called psychometrics nowadays.

Whyte described how to fit into organisations, and do well in them, people had to channel themselves into orthodox ways of thinking and behaving. There was little or no room for creative conflict. Bound by golden chains of money, benefits, perks, prestige, status and recognition in a hierarchical system in which he has already invested a great deal of time and emotional energy, the organisation man (women didn't count those days) was a willing captive. He became a 'yes man'. Whyte felt that this represented a diminishing of human life: 'The peace of mind offered by organisations remains a surrender, and no less for being offered in benevolence'.

Has all this gone away? Has the organisation man or woman disappeared? Professor Matts Alvesson doesn't think so. He coined the phrase 'functional stupidity' to describe a 'socially supported lack of reflexivity, substantive

---

17   William H. Whyte Jr., *The Organization Man* (Jonathan Cape, 1957), 173.
18   Vance Packard also drew attention to this in *The Hidden Persuaders* (1957) where he quotes the example of Armco Steel Corporation who tested 20,000 employees and claimed they had reduced from 5 per cent to 1 per cent the number of new employees with 'undesirable or borderline personality faults'. How that 1 per cent got on we will never know! Vance Packard, *The Hidden Persuaders* (Penguin Books, 1972), 169.

meaning and justification'.[19] He sees this at work in organisations where avoidance of doubt and reflection leads to shallow beliefs, to conformist acceptance rather than questioning and challenging. He describes how people possessing functional stupidity are often socially smooth, quick climbers of career ladders. He cites authoritarian regimes, groupthink, routine work and charismatic leaders as prime causes of functional stupidity.

The turn towards Motivational Communication, that took place from the 1980s onwards, ushered in a new language of 'vision', 'mission' and 'values' – a new corporate catechism. All this was well intentioned. It represented a concerted attempt to give employees a higher sense of purpose and equip them with codes of behaviour that would help the organisational culture to become more coherent and successful. But it's no coincidence that words like vision and mission have strong religious overtones. They represent an attempt to inculcate popular beliefs and behaviours amongst employees, just as missionaries used religious propaganda to change the behaviour of pagans. This fashion will not last although it seems set in at the moment. Visions and missions never did have much credibility for ordinary employees who have limited opportunities to voice their real opinions on such things.

And anyway, visions, missions and values should not be handed down on tablets of stone by management committees, or even worse, charismatic leaders. Of course it is important to have shared values, particularly when it comes to ethics, but they should not be static. Even the original proponents of setting values were honest enough to see the limitations. They said: 'Even if ultimate values are chimerical, particular values clearly make sense for specific organisations operating in specific economic circumstances'.[20] There's the problem. In an ever more diverse world, moving faster and faster and increasingly interconnected, it doesn't make sense to have a fixed system of values, you need one that's constantly kept under review. Instead of having visions, it would be better to have clear, revisable goals; instead of missions, a plainly stated core purpose with a social dimension.

There are a couple of other types of propaganda to watch out for in organisations. Remember the fashion for the charismatic leader – the Moses that would lead employees to the Promised Land? They're slightly less fashionable now since the crash of 2008 proved so many of them to be hollow

---

19 Matts Alvesson, *The Triumph of Emptiness* (Oxford University Press, 2013), 216.
20 Terrence Deal and Allen Kennedy, 'Values: The Core of the Culture', in Andrew Campbell and Kiran Tawadey (eds), *Mission and Business Philosophy* (Butterworth-Heinemann, 1992), 108.

inside. Let's hope that particular management fad has passed. It's redolent of an era when you could observe an:

> obsessional crowd ... chained to the charisma of a leader who provides the meaning of life, the logic, the value system, the images of purity and cleansing, the mystical channelling and ordering that eliminates uncertainty and doubt.[21]

Start worrying if pictures of your CEO start appearing all over the organisation. Charismatic leaders have no place in the PROGRESSIVE ORGANISATION with its emphasis on collaborative, distributed leadership.

Then there's the possible introduction of 'nudging' into organisational communication. Popularised by Richard Thaler's book in 2008,[22] 'nudging' techniques have been unashamedly adopted by a government propaganda unit that, until recently, was in Downing Street.[23] 'Nudges' enlist automatic psychological responses – the rules of thumb that help you make quick decisions. The philosophy behind nudging is apparent in this comment:

> Social practices, and the laws that reflect them, often persist not because they are wise but because humans, often suffering from self-control problems, are simply following other humans. Inertia, procrastination, and intuition often drive our behaviour.

Nudging is called 'libertarian paternalism' and it follows naturally in the wake of welfare paternalism and intellectual paternalism. This is an invisible, even insidious form of propaganda run by 'choice architects' who have decided what's good for you (or them).

It's easy for internal communication to slip gently into the comforting warm bath of mild propaganda. Principled Persuasion stops this process dead by creating new infrastructures of collaborative communication with employees. Propaganda only works when the dominant form of communication is top down. Once all employees are well informed, and have a chance to have their say not once a year but all the time, the old techniques of Motivational Communication will die out.

---

21 Elisabeth Young-Bruehl, *The Anatomy of Prejudices* (Harvard University Press, 1996), 240.
22 Richard H. Thaler and Cass R. Sunstein, *Nudge: Improving Decisions about Health, Wealth and Happiness* (Yale University Press, 2008), 238.
23 See www.gov.uk/government/organisations/behavioural-insights-team

The Principles of Truthful Persuasion

Postmodernists believed that, in the twenty-first century, organisations would move towards having no clear centres of power or even spatial locations. Their cultures would be dominated by paradox, extreme flexibility, diversity and even disorganisation. The metaphor for such organisations would move from being fixed buildings or mechanical structures to something more like a cloud. Some of this is beginning to happen. There's plenty 'in the cloud' these days. Some organisations are responding to the need not just to 'involve employees', but to make them central to a collaborative system of distributed management. Communication must adjust to this new way of working.

Here are some differences between Motivational Communication and Principled Persuasion.

Motivational Communication	Principled Persuasion
Led by management's needs	Responding to workforce needs
Aiming to control	Setting people free
Aiming to motivate performance	Nurturing a happy environment
Replete with general statements	Specific messages on specific issues
Setting out the way of thinking	Stimulating discussion and debate
Creating the perspective	Asking people for new perspectives
Promoting uniformity	Reflecting diversity

All the elements in the Motivational Communication list are self-evidently akin to propaganda. They are all aimed at projecting management's aims onto the organisation and reflect 'power from above'. With Principled Persuasion, the emphasis is on difference, individuality, exchange of ideas, entrepreneurship and more freedom for individuals to discover truths for themselves. Principled Persuasion draws on 'power from below'. Here are the Principles of Truthful Persuasion.

Principle 1: Communicate with maximum openness and transparency

Employees are quick to realise when they are not being told the whole truth. Avoid exaggerations and other distortions. Eliminate misinformation and disinformation. Some commercial secrets are necessary, but far fewer than supposed. Ask yourself, why aren't we telling employees more about our markets, our competitors, impending threats and opportunities?

Principle 2: Tap into a plurality of perspectives

The more diverse the lifestyles and cultures within the workforce, the richer it is as a source of information and ideas. Diversity in leadership teams is crucial too. You need individuals approaching issues from different directions. The communication infrastructure should provide opportunities and encouragement for a continuous stream of different perspectives, not only on specific tasks and problems, but also on the organisation's values, aims and core purpose.

Principle 3: Provide full explanations of decisions made

Leaders should see themselves as accountable to their employees. No longer controllers, in the PROGRESSIVE ORGANISATION leaders are catalysts for the creation of good ideas throughout the workforce. They should provide everyone with access to top-level thinking and decision-making.

Principle 4: Tell the truth about the changing workplace

Alert employees to the major trends affecting the world of work. Help them put their experiences into context with what's happening across the globe. Treat them as mature adults who are quite capable of assessing bad news providing they understand the background. Acknowledge the unpredictability of events and human behaviour. Remember, truth breeds trust.

By following the Principles of Truthful Persuasion, organisations can create a community of work that's much more like the society in which employees live. The change in perspective is considerable. Where you saw strange differences before, you now see diversity; where once you saw inferiority, you recognise the need for education and training; where you used to look for the Truth, you now rejoice in the fact that there are many truths.

PART IV

NEXT STEPS

CHAPTER 10

Make the Right Moves: Practical Steps Towards a Progressive Organisation Nurtured by Principled Persuasion

The only happy people I know are the ones working well at something they consider important.[1]

So what next? In practical terms, what moves do you need to make to change from being a Motivational Communicator to a Principled Persuader? How can you, personally, contribute to the creation of a PROGRESSIVE ORGANISATION? In what ways can you turn your current job into a role that is far more central to the organisation's success? How do you take those first steps towards the C-Suite?

Task number one is to make an assessment of your own organisation in terms of whether it is ENGINEERED or PROGRESSIVE. Here are two descriptions of organisations at opposite poles. What elements do you recognise?

The highly ENGINEERED ORGANISATION is one where the mindset of its leaders is still firmly rooted in the concept of command and control. Employees are seen as disposable human resources. Managers are expected to use technology to exert detailed control over employee actions. Everyone is closely monitored. Compliance and conformity are demanded at all levels. Its only constraints are legal, not ethical. The idea of empathy or compassion is laughed at. The culture is prescribed, employees are 'aligned' with it. People

---

1   A.H. Maslow, 'Additional Notes on Self-Actualisation, Work, Duty, Mission', in *Maslow on Management* (John Wiley & Sons, 1998).

are frightened to express their true thoughts and feelings. Criticism is seen as opposition. Lip service prevails. People keep their heads down. Employees are encouraged to be aggressively competitive. They are only given the information and training deemed necessary to do their jobs. Bad people and bad interpersonal practices thrive in nooks and crannies. The main aim of internal communication is to exhort people to be more committed and work harder, although this is often disguised in sweet language.

The highly PROGRESSIVE ORGANISATION achieves success by prioritising good communication. It is sensitive and responsive to the needs and wants of its employees. It sees them as a community of responsible, diverse individuals, each with a particular contribution to make. It wants them to enjoy their work. It wants to hear their ideas and concerns. It encourages employees to make connections with each other and converse. In fact, there's a real buzz in the organisation due to continuous dialogues. Its ethical foundations are strong and kept under review by employees. Technology is used to increase the knowledge and understanding of employees. Transparency and openness is the norm. Trust levels are high. Continuous feedback from employees provides insights and checks on the performance of the organisation. The main aim of internal communication is to create a caring culture where employee happiness is maximised, harm is minimised and individuals feel it's possible for them to find personal fulfilment through their work.

Your organisation is almost certainly somewhere between these two poles. It will probably contain elements of both. If the description of the highly ENGINEERED ORGANISATION fits perfectly, you should try and get another job. That's because it's only going to get worse. New computer business systems are coming on line all the time that have the capacity to pin employees down in a way that Frederick Winslow Taylor would have envied. If you look around the world, you can already see organisations using new software programmes to turn their employees into human robots.[2] In due course, they will replace them with the real thing.

Anyway, let's assume you have some room for manoeuvre – that you want to begin putting some ideas forward that will take your organisation in a more progressive direction. You would like to become a Principled Persuader whose overall strategic aim is not to 'motivate' or 'engage' employees but to create a working culture that frees them up to flourish as individuals. What's more, you want to help shape the future of the whole organisation.

---

2   For a discussion on this, see Simon Head, *Mindless: Or Why Smarter Machines are Making Dumber Humans* (Basic Books, 2014).

Strategy, Strategy, Strategy

Principled Persuaders should be, above all else, strategic thinkers. Organisations have long recognised the strategic importance of external communication, but have failed to give internal communication the same level of priority. This is partly because of the way internal communication has evolved, as a subset of HR, PR or marketing departments. It's also partly because even HR is only used strategically by around 30 per cent of British organisations, and even then its emphasis is on creating a high performance workplace.[3] Employee communication has too often been narrowly regarded as a way of doing the minimum necessary to keep employees 'onside' with objectives set by senior management. It's time to change all this. But the only way to change it is to prove to senior management that internal communication, in the form of Principled Persuasion, is a core strategic competence. So here are the essential components of Principled Persuasion strategy.

1. *Twenty-first century strategy* will involve a shift away from long-term planning towards the creative management of continuous and unpredictable change. While highly ENGINEERED ORGANISATIONS will inevitably head as fast as they can towards the replacement of humans by robots, organisations that continue to employ people will need to find ways of enhancing those skills that are unique to humanity. Communication and interconnectivity will be at the heart of twenty-first century strategy. No one person, or even group of people, can be expected to have the intelligence and foresight needed to chart a steady course through the turbulent winds of change. Instead, more interactive, more ethical communication is needed in every direction – to and from customers, suppliers, influencers, the global public – and those people who make everything happen in organisations, employees. This kind of communication needs organising, not controlling.

2. *Interconnectivity* produces more dialogue and debate, from person to person and group to group. The Principled Persuader's strategic role in this context is twofold: first, to work with IT experts to ensure maximum connectivity between all parts of the organisation. The emphasis should be on enabling information and conversation

---

3   Michael White, Stephen Hill, Colin Mills and Deborah Smeaton, *Managing to Change? British Workplaces and the Future of Work* (Palgrave Macmillan, 2004), 179.

to flow into easily accessed channels of communication. The communication infrastructure should allow pockets of knowledge and topical issues to be clustered intelligently so people can both learn from, and contribute to, the discussions. Second, the Principled Persuader should be promoting a culture of empathy, encouraging employees to engage in rigorous debate in a positive and collaborative fashion. The point is not to agree, or be agreed with, but to work the arguments through.

3.   *Innovation* stems from making unexpected connections. It also comes from the aggregate effect of many small improvements. Either way it is enabled by interconnectivity. Principled Persuaders can help stimulate innovation first by using Big Data techniques to measure the degree of connectivity within the organisation, and fill gaps; second, by encouraging employees to go foraging for new connections between different disciplines, skills and geographies. Encourage groups to form, discuss, decide and disband.

4.   *Information* needs to be constantly fed into all parts of the organisation to stimulate debate and discussion. The Principled Persuader's role is to provide access to knowledge from within and outside the organisation. Working with knowledge management experts, the Principled Persuader can develop a knowledge map of the organisation to help decide what fields of knowledge need to be strengthened. Where can employees get access to relevant articles or short, explanatory videos? How can internal search engines be developed to provide employees with the right information at the right time? Employees should also have access to more information on the big picture stuff such as trends in markets and social attitudes. Trust them to decide what's relevant to their work at any particular time. Treat employees as being able to deal with complexity – don't oversimplify.

5.   *The continuous education* of employees is a hallmark of PROGRESSIVE ORGANISATIONS. They understand that thinking in one area can stimulate thinking in another. Principled Persuaders should find out what employees want to learn and source the appropriate educational suppliers. Conduct a review of the latest online learning services and make them easily available. Send out a message that more time for learning will be built into employees' personal objectives. The strategic value of educating employees lies in opening minds and

encouraging new perspectives. This promotes diversity of thought that, in turn, produces more new connections and innovations.

6. *Mentalisation* is a new and unfamiliar subject for internal communication. Its strategic value lies in a chain of events: higher awareness of the roles of beliefs, attitudes and emotions will help employees become more self-monitoring and mindful of their behaviour towards others; this will improve interpersonal communication and collaboration; collaborative behaviour is of the highest strategic importance to the PROGRESSIVE ORGANISATION. The Principled Persuader should find ways of communicating the basics of psychology to get people thinking about the way they think. The latest developments and insights from psychology and neuroscience can be summarised and the implications explained.

7. *Analysis* of the content of communication flows around the organisation, especially from continuous feedback forums, will produce insights and information useful to top-level decision-making. The development of Happiness and Harm profiles will provide new metrics of the organisation's mental and physical health. Analysis of the use of language throughout the organisation will keep a finger on the pulse of employees' thoughts and emotions. Rigorous use of analytics will prove that Principled Persuasion is not a 'soft' discipline.

8. *Communication skills* will be high on the strategic agenda of PROGRESSIVE ORGANISATIONS. Principled Persuaders will be at the forefront of a drive to teach employees how to have more productive conversations, discussions and debates. Presentation and public speaking skills will become an essential requirement for all personnel involved in talking to groups. The vast majority of managers would agree that communication and influencing skills are essential for good management today. It's really quite amazing that training in communication skills hasn't already become a high priority for most organisations.

Building a Network

One person, however talented, can't be expected to put all these different parts of the strategy in place. In due course, just as there are teams of finance, marketing and HR specialists, PROGRESSIVE ORGANISATIONS will build teams of Principled Persuaders. But even the longest journey has to begin with a single step. Having defined the role of Principled Persuasion in strategic terms, the next step is to start putting together a network of experts to help you make the right moves. These experts can come from within the organisation and from suppliers. You may have one or more of the skills below yourself. You're going to need:

- IT consultants to help construct new channels of communication and a web of interconnectivity.
- Experts in knowledge management to create a knowledge map of the organisation and more open access to information.
- Researchers able to analyse continuous streams of feedback and present findings graphically.
- Advisors in online and other forms of educational programmes.
- Psychologists, in touch with the latest trends in neuroscience.
- Counsellors in mental and physical health to provide services direct to employees.
- Access to ethics managers or teachers to help develop employee forums on ethics and communicate ethical principles.
- Text analysts who can use Big Data techniques to explore vocabulary, metaphor and sentiment within the organisation.
- Trainers in the communication skills of conversation, presentation, debate, public speaking and expressive writing.
- HR colleagues to provide advice and data.

All this is based on the premise that Principled Persuasion is a distinctly different discipline from any other. At the moment, the closest to what's described above is most likely to be in the human resources department. However, by making the right moves now, internal communicators can begin the process of creating a new strategic internal communications hub, that will prove its importance as the twenty-first century unfolds. Right now though, to make all this happen, another step is needed. You'll have to convince senior managers that this is the right way to go.

Convincing Your Bosses

You won't get anywhere without some support from senior level management. Just as they're getting used to the idea of spending money on annual employee surveys and some communication material, you're now telling them it's time to move on and develop a far more comprehensive internal communication infrastructure. Some of the more far-sighted leaders may not need a lot of convincing. Others, still entrenched in twentieth-century mindsets, may struggle to see the benefits. In either case you need to put forward a persuasive presentation. Let them know in advance what the presentation is about, and that you'll be asking for more money to support a medium-term strategic plan. Here are some tips to help you to put this presentation together.

- Keep the presentation simple and pitched at a strategic level – draw a big picture and relate what you're saying to your organisation's core purpose.
- Describe the long-term aim of creating a progressive culture in terms that make sense to your organisation.
- Show evidence for the link between happy, involved employees and organisational success.
- Explore the way the workplace will change in the next decade, drawing on this book and other sources.
- Using existing survey material, show how employees have an appetite for more voice, more involvement.
- Put the case for dropping the increasingly outdated annual opinion survey in favour of new channels of real time feedback from employees.
- Show how new metrics, in the form of Happiness and Harm profiles, can be created (gather data beforehand to show how possible this is).
- Show the advantages of the Principled Persuasion way of proceeding and the downsides of not doing so – create a new perspective.
- Conclude by suggesting some manageable first steps, not too costly, but ones that fit in with current organisational strategy, and where the impact is measurable.
- Keep your tone of voice positive, optimistic and forward-looking. Tell the truth as you see it.
- Avoid clichés and jargon – choose suitable metaphors, short memorable phrases and use attractive visuals.
- Think hard about the issues most likely to be in your bosses' minds – what questions are they likely to ask? What emotions are they likely to feel? Be prepared for robust challenges.

These are just tips. You will have your own way of pulling a presentation together. But what really matters is that you're moving forward. Not content to keep rehashing old ideas, you want to begin experimenting and finding better ways of creating a working culture that's fit for the twenty-first century. Reinforce your arguments with suitable quotes from independent commentators. How about: 'A critical factor of leadership is to embrace the plurality of opinions – of diverging worldviews – in order to have a better chance of making sense of the future.'[4] Or more challengingly: 'Diversity can no longer be a buzzword. It must become an active search for the idiosyncratic and peculiar, the weird and the kooky, the colourful and bizarre.'[5]

So, Are You Making Progress?

The idea of growth is central to the idea of progress. Augustine thought that the cultural progress of the human race could be compared to the growth and development of an individual through education. The world now has far more educated people than it ever had before, so that must be progress? Yet, as I've argued throughout this book, too many organisations are failing to enable their employees to make progress in the way it really matters. Too many employees are caught up in a working environment that provides them with some means for living, but not much else. It just doesn't make sense to keep going in that direction.

Machiavelli thought there was no such thing as progress. He said the combination of humanity's dark side, and the random nature of events, produces a continuous struggle, not a way forward. And that does accurately describe the situation for many employees trudging away on the hedonic treadmill, but getting nowhere. There has to be a way to turn work into both a productive and a pleasurable activity for the vast majority of employees. Technology is not the answer to this. It can work to entrap or liberate. It all depends on the attitudes of the people currently in charge and of the generation that succeeds them.

Since the 1970s, books on management have been predicting hierarchies will collapse into networks, employees will flit happily from job to job enjoying 'portfolio careers', working hours will shorten to give more leisure time, routine work will be replaced by knowledge work. Now, nearly 50 years on, where are we? The hierarchies are flatter but still there. There's not enough training and hardly any education for employees. Working hours are longer not shorter. Low paid, low skilled employees are still engaged in mind-numbing routine work, kept in line by managers and technologies using targets and sanctions instead of whips.

---

4   Richard Watson and Oliver Freeman, *Futurevision: Scenarios for the World in 2040* (Scribe, 2012), 17.
5   Gary Hamel, *The Future of Management* (Harvard Business School Press, 2007), 175.

To add insult to injury, organisations that reward loyalty by getting rid of employees to 're-engineer', 'downsize' or merge; that put them under pressure to work 'flexibly', that is, uncertain hours; that keep their noses to the grindstone and think of any non-job related activity during working hours as 'time-theft'; that keep wages down to the minimum often relying on the state to subsidise them through welfare; organisations like these call on their employees to become 'more engaged' and somehow think that positive, motivational communication will increase their productivity.

No wonder so many employees refuse to reward their organisations with loyalty they know won't be reciprocated; no wonder so many withdraw emotionally from their work; no wonder they put up a shield of cynicism, resentment and apathy to protect themselves. Yet economists continue to scratch their heads and wonder why national productivity is not improving, as it should be. All they need to do is look around them. People are yearning for more enjoyable work. In research, 78 per cent of men and women say that 'really enjoying my job' is far more important than any other factor.[6]

Principled Persuasion can't solve all these problems but it can make a huge contribution to steering workplace cultures in the right direction. At its heart lie the concepts of fairness and social justice. In its head lies the calculation that unless work environments change radically, the best people will gravitate to a minority of PROGRESSIVE ORGANISATIONS. Meanwhile, the rest will have to content themselves with working under outdated management methods, doing as little as they have to do to get through the day.

What the organisational world most needs to drive it forward is constant innovation. That's where the productivity increases and the biggest improvements in products and services will come from. Constant innovation will only be achieved if all employees are enabled and educated to take part in a democracy of ideas, in a working environment where happiness is maximised, harm is minimised and ethics are a reflection of the employees' own ideas about what is good and right.

It's Up to You

Throughout this book there has been an emphasis on the need for higher levels of personal responsibility in the workplace. The authentic life is lived by being

---

6   Kate Holmes, *The Future of Work: Individuals and Workplace Transformation* (Equal Opportunities Commission, 2007), viii.

true to your deepest beliefs and principles. Everyone has a choice of whether to take action or not. My belief is that there are many wise and good professional communicators who would like to contribute to making a better world. The pathways to the future, opened up by Principled Persuasion, provide you with an opportunity to take the first steps, however small, towards a more enlightened workplace.

Index

If you have found this book useful you may be interested in other titles from Gower

Cyberconnecting
The Three Lenses of Diversity
Priya E. Abraham
9781409434467 (hardback)
9781409434474 (e-book – PDF)
9781472403629 (e-book – ePUB)

The Culture Builders
Leadership Strategies for Employee Performance
Jane Sparrow
9781409437246 (paperback)
9781409437253 (e-book – PDF)
9781409483922 (e-book – ePUB)

Decision Sourcing
Decision Making for the Agile Social Enterprise
Dale Roberts and Rooven Pakkiri
9781409442479 (hardback)
9781409442486 (e-book – PDF)
9781409473640 (e-book – ePUB)

Exploring Internal Communication
Towards Informed Employee Voice
Kevin Ruck
9781472430670 (paperback)
9781472430687 (e-book – PDF)
9781472430694 (e-book – ePUB)

The Digital Renaissance of Work
Delivering Digital Workplaces Fit for the Future
Paul Miller and Elizabeth Marsh
9781472437204 (paperback)
9781472437211 (e-book – PDF)
9781472437228 (e-book – ePUB)

GOWER